The Fatimids
and their Traditions of Learning

The Institute of Ismaili Studies
Ismaili Heritage Series, 2
General Editor: Farhad Daftary

Previously published title:
Paul E. Walker, *Abū Yaʿqūb al-Sijistānī: Intellectual Missionary* (1996)

The Fatimids and their Traditions of Learning

Heinz Halm

I.B.Tauris *Publishers*
LONDON • NEW YORK
in association with
The Institute of Ismaili Studies
LONDON

Published in 1997 by I.B.Tauris & Co Ltd
6 Salem Road, London W2 4BU
175 Fifth Avenue, New York NY 10010
www.ibtauris.com

in association with The Institute of Ismaili Studies
42–44 Grosvenor Gardens, London SW1W 0EB
www.iis.ac.uk

In the United States of America and in Canada distributed by
St Martins Press, 175 Fifth Avenue, New York NY 10010

Reprinted in 2001

ISBN 1 86064 313 2

A full CIP record for this book is available
from the British Library
A full CIP record for this book is available
from the Library of Congress

Library of Congress catalog card: available

Typeset in Monotype Baskerville by Philip Armstrong, Sheffield
Printed and bound in Great Britain
by MPG Books Ltd, Bodmin

The Institute of Ismaili Studies

The Institute of Ismaili Studies was established in 1977 with the object of promoting scholarship and learning on Islam, in the historical as well as contemporary contexts, and a better understanding of its relationship with other societies and faiths.

The Institute's programmes encourage a perspective which is not confined to the theological and religious heritage of Islam, but seeks to explore the relationship of religious ideas to broader dimensions of society and culture. The programmes thus encourage an interdisciplinary approach to the materials of Islamic history and thought. Particular attention is also given to issues of modernity that arise as Muslims seek to relate their heritage to the contemporary situation.

Within the Islamic tradition, the Institute's programmes seek to promote research on those areas which have, to date, received relatively little attention from scholars. These include the intellectual and literary expressions of Shiʿism in general, and Ismailism in particular.

In the context of Islamic societies, the Institute's programmes are informed by the full range and diversity of cultures in which Islam is practised today, from the Middle East, South and Central Asia and Africa to the industrialised societies of the West, thus taking into consideration the variety of contexts which shape the ideals, beliefs and practices of the faith.

These objectives are realised through concrete programmes and activities organised and implemented by various departments of the Institute. The Institute also collaborates periodically, on a programme-specific basis, with other institutions of learning in the United Kingdom and abroad.

The Institute's academic publications fall into several distinct and interrelated categories:

1. Occasional papers or essays addressing broad themes of the relationship between religion and society in the historical as well as modern contexts, with special reference to Islam.
2. Monographs exploring specific aspects of Islamic faith and culture, or the contributions of individual Muslim figures or writers.
3. Editions or translations of significant primary or secondary texts.
4. Translations of poetic or literary texts which illustrate the rich heritage of spiritual, devotional and symbolic expressions in Muslim history.
5. Works on Ismaili history and thought, and the relationship of the Ismailis to other traditions, communities and schools of thought in Islam.
6. Proceedings of conferences and seminars sponsored by the Institute.
7. Bibliographical works and catalogues which document manuscripts, printed texts and other source materials.

This book falls into category five listed above.

In facilitating these and other publications, the Institute's sole aim is to encourage original research and analysis of relevant issues. While every effort is made to ensure that the publications are of a high academic standard, there is naturally bound to be a diversity of views, ideas and interpretations. As such, the opinions expressed in these publications must be understood as belonging to their authors alone.

Ismaili Heritage Series

A major Shiʿi Muslim community, the Ismailis have had a long and eventful history. Scattered in many regions of the world, in Asia, Africa, and now also in the West, the Ismailis have elaborated diverse intellectual and literary traditions in different languages. On two occasions they had states of their own, the Fatimid caliphate and the Nizari state of Iran and Syria during the Alamut period. While pursuing particular religio-political aims, the leaders of these Ismaili states also variously encouraged intellectual, scientific, artistic and commercial activities.

Until recently, the Ismailis were studied and judged almost exclusively on the basis of the evidence collected or fabricated by their enemies, including the bulk of the medieval heresiographers and polemicists who were hostile towards the Shiʿis in general and the Ismailis among them in particular. These authors in fact treated the Shiʿi interpretations of Islam as expressions of heterodoxy or even heresy. As a result, a 'black legend' was gradually developed and put into circulation in the Muslim world to discredit the Ismailis and their interpretation of Islam. The Christian Crusaders and their occidental chroniclers, who remained almost completely ignorant of Islam and its internal divisions, disseminated their own myths of the Ismailis, which came to be accepted in the West as true descriptions of Ismaili teachings and practices. Modern orientalists, too, have studied the Ismailis on the basis of hostile sources and the fanciful occidental accounts of medieval times. Thus, legends and misconceptions have continued to surround the Ismailis through the twentieth century.

In more recent decades, however, the field of Ismaili studies has been revolutionized due to the recovery and study of genuine Ismaili sources on a large scale – manuscript materials which in different ways survived the mass destruction of the Fatimid and Nizari Ismaili libraries. These sources, representing diverse literary traditions produced in Arabic, Persian and Indic languages, had hitherto been secretly preserved in private collections in India, Central Asia, Iran, Afghanistan, Syria and the Yemen.

Modern progress in Ismaili studies has already necessitated a complete re-writing of the history of the Ismailis and their contributions to Islamic civilization. It has now become clear that the Ismailis founded important libraries and institutions of learning such as al-Azhar and the Dar al-ʿIlm in Cairo, while some of their learned *daʿis* or missionaries developed unique intellectual traditions amalgamating their theological doctrines with a diversity of philosophical traditions in complex metaphysical systems. The Ismaili patronage of learning and extension of hospitality to non-Ismaili scholars was maintained even in such difficult times as the Alamut period when the community was preoccupied with its survival in an extremely hostile milieu.

The Ismaili Heritage Series, published under the auspices of the Department of Academic Research and Publications of The Institute of Ismaili Studies, aims to make available to wide audiences the results of modern scholarship on the Ismailis and their rich intellectual and cultural heritage as well as certain aspects of their more recent history and achievements.

Contents

Preface

When I entered the University of Tübingen in 1969, in search of a subject for my *Habilitation* – the second dissertation required by the German university system – I came across a corpus of Arabic manuscripts that had just been acquired by the university library. This collection consisted of thirty-eight manuscripts by Ismaili authors of various periods, from the North African al-Qāḍī al-Nuʿmān, who died in Cairo in 974 AD, to the Indian Bohora Amīnjī b. Jalāl (d. 1602) and ʿAbd al-Ṭayyib b. Dāwūd b. Quṭb Shāh (d. 1631). This vast panorama of Ismaili thought fascinated me from the very start, the more so since these writings gave me an insight into a hitherto unknown intellectual world. Until then, such authors as Abū Ḥātim al-Rāzī, Abū Yaʿqūb al-Sijistānī or Ḥamīd al-Dīn al-Kirmānī had been known to me at best by name, and I had had no conception of the wealth of their ideas. The most exciting experience for me, however, was the discovery that far from being a rigid dogmatic system, Ismaili thought manifested a highly impressive evolution, always keeping abreast of contemporary developments. The result of this first encounter with Ismaili literature was a study on the 'Cosmology and Soteriology of Early Ismailism', which was presented to the University of Tübingen in 1975 and appeared in print in 1978.

The study of such authors as al-Qāḍī al-Nuʿmān, Aḥmad al-Naysābūrī, al-Kirmānī, al-Mu'ayyad al-Shīrāzī and Nāṣir-i Khusraw inevitably led me to concern myself with the Fatimid caliphs, in whose circuit and services they had all been active. The brilliance and fame of this historic era was the second fascinating discovery of my Ismaili studies, and the desire to elicit the achievements of this period has since been the primary aim of my work as a scholar. This has admittedly proved a difficult venture, for the situation of sources is anything but encouraging. Although there lived at the court of the Fatimid caliphs – first at Mahdiyya and Manṣūriyya near Qayrawān (today's Tunisia), and later in Cairo – a number of chroniclers and annalists who reported events from close quarters and with inside knowledge, none of their works have fully survived; of some of them we know nothing but the title. The only exception is 'The Commencement of the Mission' (*Iftitāḥ al-daʿwa*) by al-Qāḍī al-Nuʿmān, describing – though on the basis of an earlier source – the foundation of the Fatimid caliphate in North Africa at the beginning of the tenth century AD. Of the biography of the first Fatimid caliph, al-Mahdī, (*Sīrat al-Imām al-Mahdī*) only fragments have come down to us in later quotations; the same is true of the work of the Egyptian chronicler Ibn Zūlāq (d. 997), who wrote biographies of Jawhar, the conqueror of Egypt, and the imam-caliph al-Muʿizz (953–975); this is equally true of the historian al-Musabbiḥī (d. 1029), who enjoyed the confidence and friendship of the imam-caliph al-Ḥākim (996–1021), and of whose extensive chronicle only one fragment has survived (in the Escorial Library near Madrid), and of the historical works of al-Quḍāʿī (d. 1062), a high official at the court of the imam-caliphs al-Ẓāhir (1021–1036) and al-Mustanṣir (1036–1094). From the time of the last Fatimids we must particularly mention Mūsā ibn al-Ma'mūn al-Baṭā'iḥī (d. 1192), the son of a Fatimid vizier and author of an Egyptian chronicle.

That none of these works is preserved in the original and in its entirety is an inestimable loss to the historian. How this has come about will be explained at the end of this book, where we will describe the lamentable fate of the Fatimids' boundlessly rich libraries. But a heritage of such wealth could not disappear without leaving a trace. Just as the reign of the Fatimids has left its marks on the mosques, city walls, portals and towers of Cairo – indeed the city of Cairo is itself a testimony to Fatimid activity – so too have its writers left their traces everywhere in Egyptian historiography. When reading Egyptian historical works from the Ayyubid (1171–1250) and Mamluk (1250–1517) periods, we constantly come across quotations, if not entire passages, from the lost works of the Fatimid period, so that modern historians can reconstruct a considerable portion of Fatimid records from the works of later compilers.

The most important among these compilers is the Egyptian al-Maqrīzī (d. 1442) to whom we are indebted for a three-volume history of the Fatimids, the 'Admonition of True Believers: Information about the Fatimid Imam-caliphs' (*Ittiʿāẓ al-ḥunafāʾ bi-akhbār al-aʾimma al-Fāṭimiyyīn al-khulafāʾ*). This chronicle is largely based on the works of the Fatimid annalists, which al-Maqrīzī still had at hand and also used in his other writings, especially in his geography of Cairo and Egypt (*al-Khiṭaṭ*, 'The City Quarters') and in his biographical encyclopaedia (*al-Muqaffā*, 'The Appendix'). Al-Maqrīzī was the first historian to recognize the importance of the Fatimids in the history of Egypt and Syria. Although a Sunni himself, he describes the Ismaili dynasty with great respect and praises it as the real founder of the Islamic–Egyptian state. To him the Fatimids are not heretic or even heterodox usurpers, but the legitimate forerunners of the Ayyubid and Mamluk sultans, a view that the modern historian can unhesitatingly adopt.

The second comprehensive medieval description of the Fatimid caliphate was also written in the fifteenth century. This was the 'Essential Information' (*'Uyūn al-akhbār*) by Idrīs 'Imād al-Dīn (d. 1468), the 19th supreme missionary (*dā'ī*) of the Musta'lī-Ṭayyibī Ismaili community of the Yemen. Idrīs's work is a history of the imamate in seven volumes (of which three have been published). It contains a wealth of genuine old material, including letters and documents which have not been preserved in any other source.

In addition, there are the works of numerous Ismaili missionaries of the Fatimid period, who will often be quoted below, as well as the contemporary works of Sunni authors – the chroniclers of Damascus, Aleppo and Baghdad – or the histories of non-Muslim writers such as the 'History of the Coptic Patriarchs' or the 'Chronicle' of the Greek–Orthodox John of Antioch (Yaḥyā al-Anṭākī, d. 1066).

Thus, despite the loss of Fatimid records, the modern historian can make use of a considerable amount of source material. Of course, the wheat will have to be sifted from the chaff, for mixed with the authentic material there is much that is unreliable. Hostile imputations and malevolent distortions and defamations by anti-Fatimid authors have for a long time tarnished the image of the Fatimids.

The caliphate of the Fatimids was not only a climax in the history of the Ismā'īliyya, but also one of the great eras in Egyptian history, and in Islamic history in general. Under the Fatimids and through their efforts, Cairo became one of the centres of Islamic culture and art, and a focus of scholarship and science. It is precisely the latter aspect that has failed to receive the scholarly attention it deserves. Hence, when the general editor of the Ismaili Heritage Series asked me to write something on this specific theme, I was happy to accept the task. The history of the intellectual and learning traditions under the Fatimids was a fresh field for myself as well, a field that I was eager to explore. I would therefore like to thank Farhad Daftary, who not only inspired this venture, but also assisted and promoted it with his profound knowledge; this book owes the essential features of its form and content to his suggestions and encouragement. I also wish to extend my special thanks to the translator, Azizeh Azodi, who has translated the German text with great skill.

Heinz Halm
Tübingen, May 1996

∞ Introduction ∞

Side by side with the Sunnis and the Twelver Shiʿis, the Ismailis constitute one of the most important communities within Islam. Their present spiritual leader, H.H. Prince Karim Aga Khan IV, is acknowledged by his followers as their 49th imam, the descendant of and legitimate successor to the Prophet Muḥammad. After a period of concealment, the Ismailis first appeared on the stage of world history around 874 AD, when their propagators and missionaries began to operate, and in less than a quarter of a century they had founded a network of communities extending from the Maghrib in the west to Sind (today's Pakistan) in the east, from the mountains of Daylam on the southern shore of the Caspian Sea to the highlands of the Yemen in the south. From the very beginning, the Ismaili missionaries came forward as teachers. Teaching and learning are the very essence of the Ismaili mission, and 'the summoner' (*al-dāʿī*), the propagator and teacher, was – after the imam – the central figure of the community. The Ismailis, who are named after their 6th imam Ismāʿīl (the eldest son of the Shiʿi Imam Jaʿfar al-Ṣādiq), originally called their doctrine the 'summons to truth' (*daʿwat al-ḥaqq*) or simply *al-daʿwa*, the summons.

The period of the Fatimid caliphs (909–1171) marked a climax in the history of the Ismailis. In the year 909 the Ismailis managed to found a caliphate in present-day Tunisia, in opposition to the Sunni caliphate of the Abbasids centred in Baghdad. The 11th imam of the Ismailis, ʿAbd Allāh al-Mahdī, was proclaimed as caliph, and his descendants established one of the most important empires in Islamic history. In 969 they succeeded in peacefully conquering Egypt, where they founded Cairo as their new capital. In 973 the 14th imam, al-Muʿizz, settled there. As a dynasty of caliphs, the Ismaili imams were called 'Fatimids' because they traced their genealogy to the Prophet Muḥammad's daughter Fāṭima and hence to the Prophet himself.

The reign of the Fatimid imam-caliphs was one of the most brilliant periods of Islamic history, both politically and in terms of its literary, economic, artistic, and scientific achievements. Indeed the scientific achievements of the period deserve to form the subject of a separate volume, for Fatimid traditions of learning have spread their influence geographically far beyond the limits of the Fatimid empire itself – as far as India and western Europe – and chronologically beyond the political end of the dynasty.

∞ ONE ∞

The Ismaili Mission and the Fatimid Caliphate

At the edge of the Syrian desert, 30 kilometres south-east of Ḥamāh, lies the small town of Salamiyya (originally Salamya, from the Greek Salamias). In the town centre, amid dark, flat houses and adjoining the remains of an old church which was transformed into a mosque in the early Islamic period, rises a large, domed building consisting of the local black volcanic stone. Inside this building is a modest tomb with an iron canopy arched over it. The attendant who has the key to this mausoleum and opens the little door to visitors willingly supplies information about the man resting here: he is 'the imam 'Abd Allāh al-Fāṭimī', the ancestor of the Fatimid caliphs of Cairo and of the Aga Khans. As the inscription on the lintel states, the building dates from the eleventh century, when the Fatimids had succeeded in consolidating their power in this part of Syria. The real tomb of their ancestor must have been lost by that time, but they paid tribute to the site which had witnessed the beginnings of their movement two centuries earlier. To this day the Ismailis of Salamiyya call the mausoleum Maqām al-Imām or 'Abode of the Imam'.[1]

The man commemorated in the black-domed chamber was called 'Abd Allāh – that is one of the few facts we know for certain. Later Fatimid tradition calls him 'Abd Allāh al-Akbar, 'the Elder', in order to distinguish him from the founder of the Fatimid dynasty, 'Abd Allāh al-Mahdī.[2] What we know about the life and destiny of this elder 'Abd Allāh stems from two entirely different sources. One is the account of Ibn Rizām, from Kūfa on the Euphrates, who wrote a pamphlet against the Ismailis in the first half of the tenth century; his work has not survived, but several later authors have quoted and preserved relatively long passages from it. The other source is the quasi-'official' Fatimid version, written by the Ismaili missionary (*dāʿī*) Aḥmad al-Naysābūrī during the reign of the caliphs al-ʿAzīz (975–996) and al-Ḥākim (996–1021). The title of Naysābūrī's booklet – 'How the Imam Concealed Himself, and How the Missionaries Dispersed into Different Regions to Look for Him' (*Istitār al-imām wa-tafarruq al-duʿāt li-ṭalabihī*) – summarizes the adventurous fate of 'Abd Allāh the Elder. It is interesting to observe that, despite its slanderous distortions and exaggerations, the information provided about 'Abd Allāh's life by the anti-Ismaili pamphleteer Ibn Rizām corresponds in its basic outlines with the Fatimid family tradition. This enables us to sift a historical core of events from the two widely differing sources.

Both sources agree that 'Abd Allāh's home was the town of 'Askar Mukram on the Dujayl River (present-day Kārūn) in the province of Khūzistān at the northern end of the Persian Gulf. In the Middle Ages, 'Askar Mukram – about 40 kilometres upstream from Ahwāz – was a flourishing economic centre with textile manufactures and sugar refineries. Today only the ruins of Band-i Qīr bear witness to its former existence. 'Abd Allāh, a wealthy merchant who owned two houses, began to spread the Ismaili doctrine from 'Askar Mukram. He is the first person who evidently sent out missionaries or propagandists (*duʿāt*, singular, *dāʿī*); in this respect too, both our sources agree. We do not know in what areas these *dāʿī*s appeared; we merely discover – again from both sources – that his doctrines met with resistance in ʿAskar Mukram itself causing ʿAbd Allāh to flee the town and go into hiding, and the destruction of his houses by his enemies. ʿAbd Allāh first went to Baṣra where he was sheltered by the clients of his family; but here too his opponents tracked him down and he had to flee again. He left Iraq and went to Syria where he apparently found refuge in a Christian convent in the hills of the Jabal al-Summāq (today's Jabal al-Zāwiya, near Maʿarrat al-Nuʿmān in northern Syria). Here his missionaries – seven of them are mentioned by name – re-established contact with him, as suggested in the title of al-Naysābūrī's book, and managed to provide the imam with a 'new identity', as we might call it today.

At this time, around 870 AD, settlers were being recruited for the ruined and ancient city of Salamiyya, now a small town. Located on the edge of the Syrian desert, it had for more than a hundred years belonged to a branch of the ʿAbbasid family who then reigned as caliphs in Baghdad. The ʿAbbasids were doing their best to revive the place and had several times brought rather large contingents of settlers there from Medina, Aleppo, Raqqa on the Euphrates, and even from distant Balkh (in present-day Afghanistan). While the missionaries were looking for a home for ʿAbd Allāh in a Syrian city, they learnt of this venture and bought a plot of land for their leader on the main street near the bazaar where he later took up residence. He continued to lead the life of a merchant and seems to have prospered in his affairs, for he soon found himself in possession of several houses. He 'tore down and built up', writes al-Naysābūrī, and finally built himself 'a towering palace' which was to become the secret centre of the Ismaili mission for the next four generations.

We do not know when ʿAbd Allāh the Elder settled down in Salamiyya, or when he died there. But it was apparently during his lifetime that the Ismaili mission in Iraq was started in the vicinity of the ruins of Babylon and present-day al-Ḥilla; the traditional dating for the foundation of this Iraqi Ismaili community is 875 or 878 AD. About his son and successor, Aḥmad, we know almost nothing except his name. A considerably later source describes him as having travelled indefatigably all over the missionary sites in Khuzistan, Iraq and Daylam (the highland south of the Caspian Sea in northern Iran) disguised as a merchant.

Aḥmad had two sons, al-Ḥusayn and Abū ʿAlī Muḥammad. In the sources, the latter also bears the enigmatic sobriquet Abuʾl-Shalaghlagh. Al-Ḥusayn is said to have lived in ʿAskar Mukram, where the family had apparently regained a foothold. Abuʾl-Shalaghlagh, however, lived in Salamiyya. When his brother al-Ḥusayn died in the year 881 or 882, Abuʾl-Shalaghlagh took his eight-year-old nephew Saʿīd (born in 873 or 874) to his home in Salamiyya and brought him up as if he were his own son, later marrying him to his daughter.[3]

This period coincides with the first successes of the Ismaili mission. In the year 881, the *dāʿī* Ibn Ḥawshab set out from Iraq for Aden with an attendant; about two years later a *dāʿī* sailed from there to Sind. From 893 on, the *dāʿī* Abū ʿAbd Allāh al-Shīʿī operated among the Berber tribes of present-day Algeria; and in 899 the *dāʿī* Abū Saʿīd al-Jannābī began his missionary activities, first on the eastern and later on the western coast of the Persian Gulf.

Muḥammad Abuʾl-Shalaghlagh appears to have died in 899, at which time his nephew and son-in-law, Saʿīd ibn al-Ḥusayn, assumed the leadership of the *daʿwa*. He is better known under his subsequent throne-name of ʿAbd Allāh (incorrectly ʿUbayd Allāh) al-Mahdī; he was the first of the Fatimid caliphs. His son ʿAbd al-Raḥmān, born in Salamiyya in 893 from his marriage with his cousin, was to become the second Fatimid caliph, al-Qāʾim.

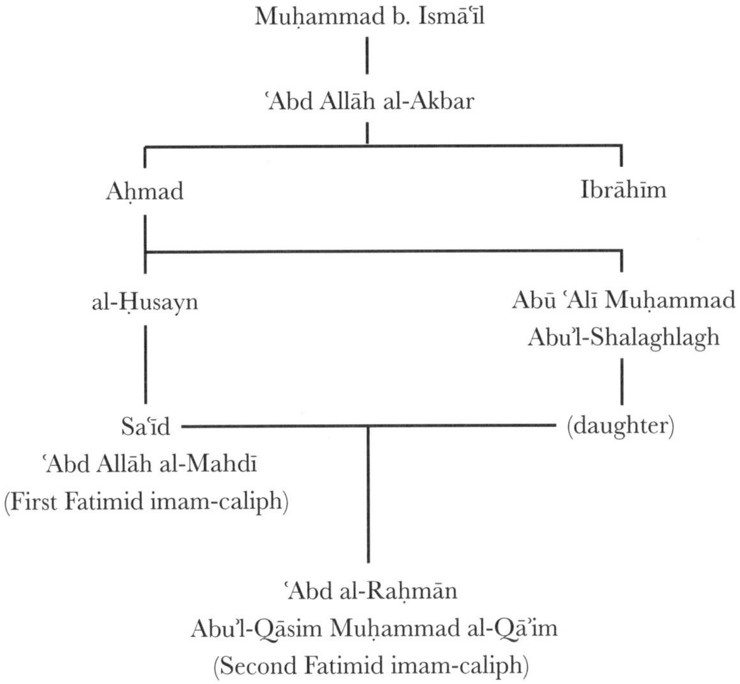

This genealogical table of the ancestors of the Fatimid caliphs and the leaders of the *daʿwa* in Salamiyya is confirmed by several sources. The point that was debated mainly in anti-Ismaili sources related to the descent and identity of ʿAbd Allāh the Elder. What we can today safely dismiss as malicious inventions are the legends circulated by Ibn Rizām al-Kūfi and his informants about ʿAbd Allāh's alleged descent from a certain Maymūn al-Qaddāḥ; in 1946 the Russian orientalist Wladimir Ivanow once and for all demolished this 'black legend'.[4]

According to the official Fatimid doctrine, and as maintained by the present-day Ismailis, ʿAbd Allah was a son of Muḥammad ibn Ismāʿīl ibn Jaʿfar al-Ṣādiq, that is a direct descendant of the Prophet Muḥammad in the eighth generation. Thus, according to Ismaili tradition, the leaders of the *daʿwa* in

Salamiyya were Fatimid ʿAlid imams. Abu'l-Shalaghlagh, however, is not considered to have been an imam; he is looked upon as a temporary representative and guardian of his nephew al-Mahdī, who is regarded as the direct successor of his father, the Imam al-Ḥusayn.

The fourth leader of the *daʿwa* residing in Salamiyya, Saʿīd ibn al-Ḥusayn, was to become the founder of one of the most important states in Islamic history under his throne-name of ʿAbd Allāh al-Mahdī. Despite some contradictions in the sources, we are quite well informed about his eventful life, above all through the autobiography of his chamberlain and foster brother of the same age, Jaʿfar al-Ḥājib, who was his faithful attendant on his flight towards the west.[5]

Al-Mahdī – as we shall call him henceforth – had continued leading the mission from Salamiyya. In the year 899, however, a schism occurred in the Ismaili community because the *dāʿīs* of Iraq, Ḥamdān Qarmaṭ and his brother-in-law, ʿAbdān, refused to acknowledge the leader in Salamiyya as their imam. Thus the 'Qarmaṭī' sect separated from the main 'Fatimid' line and thenceforth went its own way, both in religious and in political matters. When the Fatimids subsequently rose to power, they tried to win back the dissident Qarmaṭīs and make them acknowledge the Fatimid imamate. With a number of Qarmaṭī communities, especially in Iraq and Iran, these efforts appear to have been successful; only the Qarmaṭīs of Baḥrayn (eastern Arabia) persisted in rejecting the Fatimid imams.

Al-Mahdī had to face yet another difficult ordeal, this time occasioned not by his opponents but by supporters of his imamate. In the year 902 there appeared in the Syrian desert near Palmyra a number of *dāʿīs* who, apparently without authorization from Salamiyya, revealed the whereabouts of their imam and summoned the Bedouin tribes to go to Salamiyya and pay homage to him. This imprudent act was highly dangerous to al-Mahdī, who was not yet prepared for military conflict with the Abbasid caliph of Baghdad, and whose identity and residence were thus prematurely revealed to the caliph's police. Al-Mahdī secretly left Salamiyya accompanied by his small son and a few attendants, including Jaʿfar al-Ḥājib. Initially he found refuge in Ramla, the capital of the province of Palestine. Meanwhile, the Bedouins were attacked by government troops who captured their leader and forced him under torture to reveal the secret of al-Mahdī's identity. This made it impossible for al-Mahdī to remain in Palestine, so he proceeded to Egypt with his attendants. Once there he wavered between heading for the Yemen or for the Maghrib, in both of which regions there already existed important Ismaili communities. Al-Mahdī decided to go to the Maghrib. However, he preserved his anonymity and settled with his son in the Sijilmāsa oasis (today's Rissani in Morocco). This was a major city at the time and the terminal of an important route across the Sahara. As a result, many merchants from Syria and Iraq resided there, which enabled al-Mahdī to remain in the city for a few years (905–9) unrecognized in the guise of a merchant.

During this period al-Mahdī kept in close contact with the *dāʿī* Abū ʿAbd Allāh al-Shīʿī who led the mission among the Kutāma Berbers in present-day Algeria. Supported by the warlike tribes of the Kutāma, Abū ʿAbd Allāh al-Shīʿī now began the conquest of Ifrīqiya, a region covering today's Tunisia and the eastern part of Algeria. The capital of Ifrīqiya was Qayrawān (Kairouan) in Tunisia, where the emirs of the Aghlabid dynasty ruled as governors on behalf of the caliphs of Baghdad.

After years of guerrilla warfare, Abū ʿAbd Allāh al-Shīʿī succeeded in conquering one city after another in Ifrīqiya and in finally dislodging the Aghlabid emir. In March 909 the *dāʿī* led his Kutāma warriors into the palaces of the emirs in Raqqāda near Qayrawān. Preparations for the reign of the Mahdī followed without delay; new coins were minted and the immediate arrival of the new ruler was proclaimed. An army of Kutāma warriors marched to Sijilmāsa to escort the Imam al-Mahdī to Raqqāda. Upon hearing of the advance of this army, the emir of Sijilmāsa had the foreign merchant and his son, whom he correctly suspected to be the cause of these commotions, interned in two separate houses; but the threatening attitude of the *dāʿī* and his Kutāma warriors forced him to release his captives. Bathed in tears, the *dāʿī* Abū ʿAbd Allāh al-Shīʿī greeted his imam, whom he had probably only seen many years before in Salamiyya as a small child. On the following day (27 August 909) the *dāʿī* had his troops parade in front of the tent in which al-Mahdī and his son, as well as the chamberlain Jaʿfar al-Ḥājib – our eye-witness and informant – were seated, and one army unit after another paid homage to the imam-caliph. On 4 January 910 al-Mahdī, having paid a visit to the land of the Kutāma and received homage from the local tribes, entered the palace of Raqqāda. On the following day, Friday 5 January, a manifesto was read from the pulpit of the Great Mosque of Qayrawān, proclaiming 'ʿAbd Allāh Abū Muḥammad, the divinely guided commander of the faithful (*amīr al-muʾminīn al-imām al-Mahdī biʾllāh*)' as the new caliph. Al-Mahdī was thirty-five years old; according to the accounts of an eye-witness, 'his youthfulness was still complete; there was no sign of a grey hair', and his sixteen-year-old son Abuʾl-Qāsim, the future successor to the throne as al-Qāʾim, was just sprouting a moustache.

The imam-caliph and his son took up quarters in the palaces of Raqqāda, which the Aghlabid emir had left in a headlong flight. Excavated by Tunisian and French archaeologists, the ruins of Raqqāda can today be visited at some 9 kilometres south of Qayrawān. This vast site, which was once surrounded by gardens and parks, comprised several palaces, farm buildings, stables and cisterns as well as an artificial lake serving as a reservoir for drinking-water. As for nearby Qayrawān, it remained a stronghold of the Mālikī Sunnis (and a centre of opposition to the Fatimids), and was always avoided by the Fatimid caliphs.

The empire ruled by the first Fatimid caliph, ʿAbd Allāh al-Mahdī (909–934), extended from the Moroccan Atlantic coast over the entirety of present-day Algeria and Tunisia, as far as the Libyan coast of Tripolitania and Cyrenaica (Arabic, Barqa) in the east. It also included Sicily, which was conquered by the Muslims during the years 827–902. The capital of Sicily, Palermo (Arabic, Bālarm), was simply called al-Madīna or 'the city' by the Arabs. Thus the Fatimid empire was also from its very beginnings a naval power, competing with the Byzantine empire for supremacy in the Mediterranean. The major arsenals and naval bases were Tunis and, further to the south, Sousse. The capital Qayrawān and the royal city of Raqqāda, however, lay inland at some distance from the coast. This must have been the main reason for al-Mahdī's plan to found a new capital directly on the coast. He personally inspected Tunis and Carthage, but neither of these places seem to have suited him and his choice finally fell on an unsettled peninsula about 50 kilometres south-east of Sousse. This rocky peninsula was connected to the mainland by a narrow isthmus, 175 metres across, and had been settled in antiquity by a colony of Phoenician seafarers. Besides their graves, the Phoenicians had left behind a square harbour-basin artificially cut out of the flat rocks on the shore.

It was here that in the years 916–921 al-Mahdī's new royal city was built. It was called al-Mahdiyya after him, a name it has preserved to this day. The isthmus was blocked off by a mighty wall extending from shore to shore. Only a single gateway provided access to the city. The sea-wall surrounded the entire peninsula including the Phoenician harbour-basin, the approach to which could be obstructed by a chain between two watch-towers. Al-Mahdī's palace was built on the highest point of the hill; facing it somewhat further down the hill was the palace of his successor to the Fatimid throne, Abu'l-Qāsim (al-Qā'im). The strip of sandy beach (*ramla*), situated before the sea-wall, served as a praying area (*muṣallā*) for the major Islamic feasts. On the day the fast was broken at the end of Ramaḍān (*'īd al-fiṭr*) and on the feast of sacrifice (*'īd al-aḍḥā*), the imam-caliph appeared personally with his entire court to preach the sermon and lead the prayer. Further inland, in the suburbs, lived the soldiers with their families: Kutāma Berbers, Arabs, Africans and European troops from amongst the Slavs – the Africans were simply called 'Zawīla', while the Slavs were known as 'Ṣaqāliba'.

The city of Mahdiyya on the Tunisian coast is, like Cairo, one of the most important monuments of Ismaili–Fatimid history. Today the little town lives on fishing and tourism. Traces of Fatimid grandeur can still be admired everywhere: the impregnable gate, the remains of the sea-wall, the harbour basin and, on an artificially raised terrace jutting out into the sea, the mosque with its impressive portal resembling a Roman triumphal arch. Over the centuries the mosque al-Mahdī had built for himself and his retinue fell to ruins until, in the 1960s, it was completely restored and is now used once again.

Al-Mahdī died on the 4 March 934 at the age of fifty-nine. His son Abu'l-Qāsim adopted the throne-name of al-Qā'im bi-Amr Allāh ('the one who takes care of the affairs of God'). During his reign (934–946) the capital Mahdiyya experienced its worst ordeal. Several Berber tribes of the Maghrib rebelled under the leadership of a Khārijī propagandist, Abū Yazīd, who was filled with a deep hatred of Shi'i doctrines. The rebels succeeded in overrunning the whole of Ifrīqiya in the year 944, and they also occupied the city of Qayrawān. The abandoned royal city of Raqqāda was plundered and to a great extent destroyed. In January 945 the rebels blocked Mahdiyya from the land side but could not cut off its supplies by sea from Tripoli and Sicily and, since they did not have the appropriate siege engines, they were unable to conquer the capital of the Fatimid imam-caliph. On one occasion the rebel Abū Yazīd even appeared personally in front of the only gate of Mahdiyya, but was immediately forced to make a hasty retreat. According to a Fatimid legend it was for this highly dangerous moment alone that the Imam al-Mahdī had once planned the city's powerful fortifications.

For a brief time the Fatimid empire appeared to have receded to the walls of Mahdiyya itself, but then the Fatimids succeeded in breaking the blockade and preparing for a counter-attack against the Khārijī rebels. However, this breakthrough was not the work of the caliph al-Qā'im who died in May 946. His son and successor, Ismā'īl, at first kept his father's death a secret and pretended that he was still the heir to the throne; to keep up appearances he even continued to correspond with his dead father. It was not until he managed to overpower and kill the rebel Abū Yazīd in an exhausting campaign that he made himself known as the imam-caliph and assumed the appropriate throne-name al-Manṣūr ('the victorious').

The imamate of al-Manṣūr (946–953) was quite short, for he died prematurely after suffering a long illness he had contracted during his campaign. But he too left some lasting traces in addition to his military fame. After driving out the Khārijī rebels from Qayrawān in October 946 and then setting out to chase Abū Yazīd, he ordered a new royal city to be built directly to the south of Qayrawān, near the village of Ṣabra half-way towards Raqqāda. It was not until after his victory over Abū Yazīd that he was able to make his triumphal entry into this city, which he named 'al-Manṣūriyya' after himself.

From 948 to 972 Manṣūriyya was the capital city of the Fatimid empire. Excavations by archaeologists have brought to light the city's circular wall; its layout followed that of Baghdad (also founded by a caliph called al-Manṣūr), and thus emphasized the Fatimids' claim to the caliphate. The building materials were, incidentally, taken from the ruins of the palaces of nearby Raqqāda, which had been destroyed by the Khārijī hordes of Abū Yazīd.

Manṣūriyya was not only a copy of Baghdad, it was also to become a model for Cairo. Although Fatimid Cairo was built on a rectangular rather than a circular plan, the position of its gates and buildings, as well as their names, were the same as those of Manṣūriyya. Both cities had a 'Gate of Triumphs' (Bāb al-Futūḥ) through which the caliph would arrive and depart in splendid procession, and a Zawīla Gate (Bāb Zawīla in today's Cairo) named after the African units of the army. The caliph's palace was situated midway between these two gates. Nearby was the palace mosque, which bore the name 'al-Azhar', like the mosque the Fatimids later constructed in Cairo. In Manṣūriyya an aqueduct built on the Roman model supplied the city with water, which was stored in three round reservoirs. The great throne room (*al-īwān al-kabīr*) in which the imam-caliph held his audiences and received the envoys of foreign states was supported by colossal ancient columns that had been laboriously transported to Manṣūriyya by soldiers from the coastal city of Sousse. Our sources also tell us of huge stables, a menagerie of exotic animals, including a lion, and extensive gardens. The different halls bore splendid names, such as the 'Camphor Hall', the 'Crown Room', the 'Myrtle Room' and the 'Silver Hall'.

After the Fatimids moved to Egypt in the year 973 the palaces of Manṣūriyya served as residences for their viceroys from the Zīrid dynasty; but in 1053 the threat of an invasion of the Banū Hilāl Bedouins made the Zīrids return to the safer Mahdiyya on the coast. The magnificent Fatimid palaces were abandoned and left to decay. For centuries they served the population of Qayrawān as quarries, until they were finally levelled to the ground.

The fourth Fatimid imam-caliph, al-Muʿizz (953–975), spent the major part of his reign in Manṣūriyya. During his reign the Fatimid empire grew into a great power. The Maghrib was subdued in several campaigns. The nomadic Zanāta Berbers, who had made the high plateau of central Algeria unsafe, were pacified. Al-Muʿizz's freedman, Jawhar, a former 'Slav' *mamlūk*, advanced as far as the Atlantic Ocean at the head of his Fatimid army. To prove that he had actually reached the ocean he sent fish kept alive in salt-water to the imam in Manṣūriyya. In Sicily and southern Italy, Fatimid interests collided with those of the Byzantines, but the two empires succeeded in making a peaceful settlement by way of an armistice that was regularly renewed. According to this treaty the Byzantine emperor paid the imam an annual tribute, while the Fatimids agreed not to invade the mainland of Italy.

It was also from Manṣūriyya that al-Muʿizz led the extensive network of the Ismaili mission (*daʿwa*). The *dāʿīs* who were active in hostile foreign lands – in Iraq and Iran, in the Yemen and in Sind – sent their messengers each year to deliver religious dues from the different dioceses (*jazāʾir* literally, islands), as well as letters containing enquiries and reports. For safety's sake these couriers would usually travel via Mecca disguised as pilgrims, taking shelter in the anonymity of the large caravans, often made up of thousands of pilgrims, that travelled to and from the city.

In his book 'Audiences and Rides', one of our major sources of information, the supreme *dāʿī* and supreme *qāḍī* al-Nuʿmān (d. 974) very vividly describes life at the court of al-Muʿizz. From him we learn that the imam-caliph even conducted the affairs of the distant Multan (in present-day Pakistan) with his instructions. Indeed, it was al-Muʿizz who ordered the local *dāʿī* to destroy the gigantic idol of Multan which, it was thought, would tempt Muslims to relapse into polytheism.

The greatest political success of al-Muʿizz, however, was his peaceful assumption of power in Egypt in the year 969, of which more will be said in chapter three.

TWO

The Mission of the *dāʿīs* and the 'Teaching Sessions'

It is not the purpose of this book to present in detail the history of the Fatimid caliphate, which led to one of the most brilliant periods of Islamic history. The subjects to be discussed here are teaching and learning – activities that characterized the Ismaili community from its very beginnings.

Knowledge (*ʿilm*) and wisdom (*ḥikma*) are, according to Ismaili belief, gifts from God, revealed to humanity through His prophets. God has successively dispatched six prophets bearing a law (*sharīʿa*): Adam, Noah, Abraham, Moses, Jesus Christ and Muḥammad. These prophets are called 'speakers' (*nāṭiq*), because they talk to men, proclaiming to them a *sharīʿa*, an exoteric (*ẓāhir*) law with its commandments and prohibitions, its ritual obligations and legal definitions. By the side of each of these speaker-prophets stands an authorized representative (*waṣī* or *asās*) who knows and teaches the eternally immutable 'esoteric meaning' (*bāṭin*) of all these prescriptions and regulations – though only to a small number of the elect. Thus, Adam had his son Abel at his side and Noah his son Shem, Abraham's *waṣī* was his son Ishmael, Moses's *waṣī* was his brother Aaron, and Jesus Christ's was Simon Peter. The speaker-prophet of our era was Muḥammad. His *waṣī* or *asās* was his cousin and son-in-law ʿAlī ibn Abī Ṭālib. The latter's descendants are the true imams of the Islamic community (*umma*); they alone know and transmit the 'esoteric meaning' of the divine revelation proclaimed by Muḥammad. The imams, whose succession continues with the Fatimid caliphs, are thus the repositories of the divine message; they are the upholders of 'knowledge' and 'wisdom', which they transmit to their followers, the 'friends of God' (*awliyāʾ Allāh*).

The imams spread 'knowledge' and 'wisdom' through 'summoners', *dāʿī*s; these are propagators or missionaries who summon people to follow the true imam and instruct the individual who 'responds to the summons', *al-mustajīb* or the initiate, in 'wisdom'.

The missionary or *dāʿī* as a teacher is the most characteristic figure of the Ismaili movement. From the very beginning, the *dāʿī*s travelled far and wide to spread the good tidings. At first they were itinerant missionaries who, for their own protection and that of their followers, operated under the cloak of some inconspicuous profession. The first *dāʿī* of Iraq, al-Ahwāzī, earned his living as a tailor and a guardian of harvested dates; a *dāʿī* who roamed the mountains of western Syria worked as a cotton carder (*ḥallāj*), and the first missionary dispatched to the Yemen, Ibn Ḥawshab Manṣūr al-Yaman, rented a shop in the port of Aden where he traded in cotton.

The *dāʿī*s rarely appeared in public; they preferred to address specific people on their own and tried to arouse in them a curiosity about the secret teachings they had to relate. But before the adept was initiated he took an oath (*ʿahd* or *mīthāq*) by which he was solemnly sworn to secrecy. This imposed silence – a necessary precaution against religious and political enemies – naturally led to all kinds of assumptions and speculations about the Ismailis. Indeed their opponents never tired of compensating for their ignorance by freely inventing speculations and wilful defamations, which have even survived in twentieth-century literature. It is only thanks to modern scholarship, promoted by the policy of disclosure practised by the 48th imam, Sulṭān Muḥammad Shāh Aga Khan III (imamate from 1885 to 1957) and his successor, H.H. Prince Karim Aga Khan IV, that the absurd contentions and distortions circulating for centuries were clearly proved unfounded. The literature of the Ismailis is accessible today and many of the works handed down in manuscript have been printed and commented on through the joint efforts of Ismaili and Western scholars.

Even the complete wording of the oath is extant.[1] It, too, shows how groundless the insinuations of the enemies of the Ismailis have been. Through this oath the initiate solemnly binds himself to adhere to all the tenets of Islam and to carry out all the prescriptions of the *sharīʿa*. The Fatimid imams always insisted that the exoteric *ẓāhir* and the esoteric *bāṭin* be equally obligatory and binding for every believer, as long as God had not otherwise decreed. A second crucial point of the oath is the obligation to obey the true imam, whose name is not initially revealed to the disciple – again as a precaution. Absolute secrecy was another obligation; as already indicated, this was a necessity as long as the *dāʿīs* had to operate in hostile surroundings.

Once the initiate (*mustajīb*) had solemnly bound himself through the oath, he could undergo a step-by-step induction into 'wisdom' (*ḥikma*) – not all at once, for that would exceed his mental capacity. 'You are being put to a test,' the *dāʿī* would say to his disciples, 'for you are beginners, and a beginner is like an infant: you start by feeding him milk, and only later give him more nourishing food.'[2]

In an instruction for missionaries, 'On the Requisites of a Well-conducted Mission,'[3] the *dāʿī* Aḥmad al-Naysābūrī uses the same image of the infant. The initiation is carried out in three stages: the first corresponds to suckling an infant, the second to raising a child, and the third to developing the youthful mind to maturity. But the child must be sensibly nourished: 'If you feed it too much at the beginning of its existence, you will ruin it.' The *dāʿī* should therefore start by 'feeding [his disciple] with light knowledge that he is able to absorb; he should first confirm him in his recognition of the oneness of God (*tawḥīd*), in his faith in God, and in his faith in and obedience to the Prophet and the imam, for as God has said [Qur'an IV:59]: "Obey God and his envoy and those among you who are meant to command!" After that, he shall proceed to the knowledge of the other ranks.'

The relationship between teacher and pupil forms the subject of one of the oldest works of Ismaili literature, 'The Teacher and the Pupil' (*Kitāb al-ʿālim wa'l-ghulām*), which is attributed to the first *dāʿī* of the Yemen, Ibn Ḥawshab Manṣūr al-Yaman.[4] Although the plot of this 'initiation romance' is fictitious, it is certainly a faithful reflection of the practice of the earliest missionaries. Here is a summary of the story:

The teacher (*al-ʿālim*) mentioned in the title of the book is also the narrator. In an introduction – a kind of 'soliloquy'– he communes with himself about the origin of his knowledge and the duty it entails: 'I was a dead man,' he starts, 'God turned me into a living being, a learned man … Therefore it is my duty to show my gratitude for this divine grace by passing on the good entrusted to me (*amāna*) to those who will come after me, just as those who came before me have passed it on to me.' These few words contain the entire Ismaili idea of knowledge, learning and teaching. Knowledge means life; learning means resurrection from the death of ignorance; knowledge is a good entrusted by God to human beings (*amāna*) who must not selfishly keep it to themselves, but instead pass it on. Learning and teaching are a divine mission: the man who is spiritually resurrected through learning has the duty to bring his neighbour back to life as well.

In search of a worthy pupil to whom he can transmit the

good of knowledge entrusted to him, our 'teacher' travels through the world until he finally reaches a remote, secluded place in which knowledge has not yet been propagated. One evening he enters a village, mixes with a group of people discussing religious questions and takes part in their conversation. He does not directly disclose his real aim, but when it grows late and all the others go home, a young boy stays behind and desires to know more. The *dāʿī* asks the boy to dine with him, knowing that he has found his future disciple. The intelligent youth, who comes from a wealthy family, is eager to learn. He implores the teacher not to keep his knowledge to himself and anxiously asks: 'Is there a way for me to live? ... Be merciful, for you, too, were once in my present position! ... That which you call for – what is it? From whom does it come? Where does it lead?'

After this initial evening conversation, the two part, and there follows a prolonged period of preliminary discussion during which the young man is progressively led closer to the teacher's secret. Finally, the teacher reveals to him that there exists a 'key' to true knowledge, namely the oath of secrecy. The *dāʿī* reads out the formula of the oath (*kitāb al-ʿahd*) to the young man, who repeats it sentence by sentence. Thereupon, he starts teaching him the elements of religious knowledge. He explains to him the creation of the universe, points out the connection between the 'exoteric' meaning, and the inseparably correlated 'esoteric' meaning and calls his attention to the source of all knowledge, the imam as the living repository of divine truths.

Then the *dāʿī* leaves the youth alone for a time with his thoughts and doubts while he goes to see his superior and master to report on his efforts to educate the youngster. The superior is merely called *shaykh* in the text, and we do not know whether he is simply a *dāʿī* of a higher rank or perhaps the imam himself; but it hardly matters. The *shaykh* desires to meet the youngster, so the *dāʿī* returns to the village and tells the young man to pack his belongings and follow him. The latter obeys without hesitation. The prospect of acquiring knowledge is more precious than anything else to him, so he leaves his home and family to follow the teacher. The *shaykh* receives him kindly and bids his steward to provide him and his *dāʿī* with lodgings. On the following day the youngster is called before the *shaykh* and subjected to the following regular ritual of questions and answers:

Shaykh: Young man, you have been distinguished by a travelling friend, your life has been preserved by a purposeful visitor. What is your name?

Youngster: God's servant, son of God's servant [i. e., X son of Y].

Shaykh: That is your usual daily task; we have already heard about you. Are you free or a slave?

Youngster: I am a free man, the son of a servant of God.

Shaykh: Who delivered you from slavery, so that you became a free man?

Youngster: (points his finger at the wise man who has 'summoned' him): This wise man has set me free!

Shaykh: What do you think – if he himself were unfree and no master, could he have set you free?

Youngster: No, he could not have done so!

Shaykh: So what is your [real] name?

Youngster: (looks down, at a loss for an answer).

Shaykh: Young man, how can anything be known that has as yet no name, were it even a new-born baby?

Youngster: So then I was born to you: do you give me a name!

Shaykh: This will be done after a lapse of seven days.

Youngster: Why put it off for seven days?

Shaykh: For the sake of the new-born child!

Youngster: What if the new-born child should die before seven days have elapsed?

Shaykh: Nothing will befall him; after that he will receive a name.

Youngster: Will the name you will give me belong to me?

Shaykh: If you will be its servant!

Youngster: What does that mean?

Shaykh: Your name is your master in future, and you are its servant. Now cease insisting too much! Go now until the appointed day!

The pupil spends the next seven days in the company of the *dāʿī* in the *shaykh*'s house. At the end of the prescribed period he is again summoned before the *shaykh*. Having washed and put on fresh clothes he now hears from the *shaykh* 'things that the pen cannot render and the imagination cannot apprehend.' The text does not disclose to the reader what they are. The secret is preserved; it is exclusively revealed by direct personal instruction.

The act of initiation is here understood as a rebirth; the neophyte is like a new-born infant. He is given a new name and the initiation into knowledge turns him into a new man. The entrusted good (*amāna*) is now handed over to him, and it is his duty to pass on his knowledge. The *shaykh* dismisses the youngster who returns to his village. His spiritual leader, the *dāʿī*, accompanies him to the edge of the village, where he too leaves him for ever. The pupil who became an initiate has now become a teacher. He is under the obligation to pass on the good entrusted to him, that is his knowledge, and his father, who is still caught in the fetters of ignorance, will be his first pupil.

'The Teacher and the Pupil' clearly shows the high esteem the Ismailis had for learning from early on; indeed, for the Ismailis religion and learning are inseparably connected. It was the practice of the Ismaili missionaries from the very beginning of the *daʿwa* to pass on the 'wisdom' to their pupils in teaching sessions known as 'sessions of wisdom' (*majālis al-ḥikma*). A passage from the 'Book of Government' (*Siyāsat-nāma*) written by the vizier Niẓām al-Mulk (d. 1092), which refers to the earliest days of the *daʿwa* in northern Iran, provides a vivid illustration of the image of the teacher surrounded by his pupils that the Ismaili *daʿwa* presented of itself:

> One day the village elder of Kulayn [in the vicinity of today's Tehran] went outside the village. There was a ruined mosque from which he heard a voice. He went closer to the mosque to listen: it was the *dāʿī* Khalaf who was explaining the doctrine to the people.

At the other extreme of the Muslim world, in the far west, Abū ʿAbd Allāh al-Shīʿī, the first *dāʿī* in North Africa, taught his followers from the Kutāma Berber tribe in exactly the same way. Our source is the 'Book of the Commencement of the Mission' (*Kitāb iftitāḥ al-daʿwa*) by al-Qāḍī al-Nuʿmān, which is based on a biography (*sīra*), or perhaps even an autobiography of Abū ʿAbd Allāh. Several passages describe the way the *dāʿī* went about his work. At first:

> ... he would hold sessions for them and tell them the external (*ẓāhir*) advantages of ʿAlī ibn Abī Ṭālib and the imams among his descendants. When he saw how one after the other learned from him and felt that he had [the pupil] where he wanted him, he would give away one little piece after another, as long as he acquiesced, and would finally administer the oath to him.

The earliest targets of Abū ʿAbd Allāh's mission were the Banū Saktān clan, who had offered him hospitality and protection. They were the first to be initiated into the Ismaili faith in the Maghrib:

> He summoned some of the Banū Saktān; thereupon they reserved him a session (*majlis*) to hear him. Again and again he addressed admonishments to them and taught them wisdom (*ḥikma*); to this end he assembled them and sat for them most of the day. Every day he would sit for the faithful, talk to them and explain, and he

ordered the *dāʿīs* to do the same. The women, too, participated in these sessions to hear the wisdom.[5]

This is how the clans and tribes of the Kutāma people were gradually won over for the *daʿwa* and took the oath of allegiance to the Imam-Mahdi, whose name had not yet been made known. Supported by the power of his followers, the *dāʿī* was finally able, after a ten-year mission, to begin an armed revolt against the emir of Qayrawān. In the year 902, the Kutāma forced the small town of Mīla (the ancient Roman Mileu or Mileve) west of present-day Constantine to capitulate. This was the beginning of a guerrilla war against the established state power which ended seven years later with the conquest of Qayrawān. The last emir of the Aghlabid dynasty abandoned his palaces in a headlong flight and made off for Egypt. After the entrance of the *dāʿī* Abū ʿAbd Allāh al-Shīʿī into the royal city of Raqqāda on 25 March 909, the Ismaili *daʿwa* was established in nearby Qayrawān, the metropolis of Ifrīqiya. Berber *dāʿīs* trained by Abū ʿAbd Allāh assumed the mission among the Sunni population and were soon joined by many others.'[6]

One year after the fall of Qayrawān, the promised Mahdi at last appeared and took over the empire founded by the *dāʿī* Abū ʿAbd Allāh after seventeen years of persistent effort. On 4 January 910, the imam ʿAbd Allāh made his entry into the royal city of Raqqāda, accompanied by his son and the *dāʿī*, and on the following day, a Friday, he was proclaimed as the new caliph in the Great Mosque of Qayrawān. Thus began the reign of a dynasty designated by later generations as the 'Fatimids', the descendants of Fāṭima, the daughter of the Prophet, although they do not seem to have called themselves by that name. The dynasty simply called itself *dawlat al-ḥaqq*, the 'true' or 'legitimate dynasty', just as it called its mission *daʿwat al-ḥaqq*, the 'true mission'.

After the establishment of the Fatimid reign, the *daʿwa* could operate openly at least within the Fatimid sphere of influence; it was only beyond the Fatimid borders that the *dāʿīs* had to continue working clandestinely. The teaching sessions (*majālis al-ḥikma*) were now institutionalized, but of course only those who had previously taken the oath of allegiance (*ʿahd*) could participate in them.

After the *dāʿī* Abū ʿAbd Allāh was killed in February 911 he was succeeded as leading *dāʿī* by one of his most gifted pupils, a Kutāma Berber of the Malūsa tribe called Aflaḥ ibn Hārūn al-Malūsī. One of the first to follow the summons of the *daʿwa*, Aflaḥ ibn Hārūn had been sent by Abū ʿAbd Allāh to his own tribe as *dāʿī*, hence his sobriquet 'the *dāʿī* of the Malūsa'. After the establishment of the Fatimid caliphate, he first became the judge (*qāḍī*) of the city of Tripoli in Libya, and then supreme *qāḍī* of the two royal cities of Raqqāda and Mahdiyya, that is the supreme judge of the whole empire. From this time it became a tradition for the supreme judge (*qāḍī al-quḍāt*) to act at the same time as the supreme missionary (*dāʿī al-duʿāt*); *ẓāhir* and *bāṭin*, the 'external' *sharīʿa* and its 'inner' interpretation, were thus united in one and the same person. Throughout their reign, the Fatimids had emphatically insisted that the initiate should observe the external commandments of Islamic law under all circumstances; they had already been committed to do so under the oath of allegiance. The *ẓāhir* and the *bāṭin* formed an inseparable unit, embodied in the person and authority of the supreme *qāḍī* and *dāʿī*.

On the activities of the supreme *dāʿī* Aflaḥ ibn Hārūn al-Malūsī, we have some information from a source which has only been preserved in fragments in the form of quotations by later authors: the 'Biography of the Imam al-Mahdi' (*Sīrat al-Imām al-Mahdī*).[7] The author of this biography of the first Fatimid imam-caliph, a subordinate *dāʿī*, knew the supreme *dāʿī* personally, since the latter was his superior and probably his teacher as well. On the occasion of Aflaḥ's death (before 923), the pupil remembers the teaching methods of his master in the *majālis al-ḥikma*:[8]

> I listened to him while he was performing his missionary function among women and using allusions for them in his sermon that their intelligence could grasp and that impressed themselves upon them, for he used to say: 'God disposes of the appropriate argument' [Qur'an, VI:149]; it is the one with which he addresses the knowing person according to his knowledge and the unknowing person only within the limits of his understanding! He had the habit, when talking to women, to choose as examples finery or the finger-ring, the earring and diadem, necklace, anklet or bracelet, dress or scarf, spinning and weaving, hair-style, wardrobe and other things with which women adorn themselves. To the artisan he spoke about his respective trade; to the tailor, for instance, about needle and thread, eyelet and scissors; to the shepherd about his staff and wrap, and the flock and the shepherd's pouch.

Two things are remarkable in this text dating from the earliest period of the Fatimid caliphate: the first is the pedagogical skill with which the *dāʿī* adapted himself to each respective audience, and the second is the matter-of-factness with which the message of the *daʿwa* was also transmitted to women. Already Abū ʿAbd Allāh al-Shīʿī had held *majālis* for women, and to this day the culture and education of girls and women remains one of the major priorities of the Ismaili community.

The successor to Aflaḥ al-Malūsī and the third head of the *daʿwa* was al-Qāḍī al-Nuʿmān ibn Muḥammad who, like his predecessor, had first been judge of the city of Tripoli in Libya. In the year 948, the third Fatimid imam-caliph, al-Manṣūr (946–953), appointed him as the supreme judge and chief missionary. Al-Nuʿmān, a jurist of Arab origin, was the founder of the Ismaili school of jurisprudence (*madhhab*); his main work, the 'Pillars of Islam' (*Daʿāʾim al-Islām*), remains the classic of this school.[9] Like his two predecessors, he also united in his hand the knowledge and doctrine of both the *ẓāhir* and the *bāṭin*; his numerous writings contain information about both.

The 'external' (*ẓāhir*) law, the *sharīʿa*, according to the Ismaili school of jurisprudence (*madhhab*), was accessible to all Muslims, for it was the legal basis for the daily life of all. But as it was new – the Qāḍī al-Nuʿmān himself had compiled it from the Shiʿi tradition – it had to be made known to the people. This was done in public teaching sessions held by the Qāḍī al-Nuʿmān each Friday after the Friday prayer, that is, between the midday prayer (*ẓuhr*) and the afternoon prayer (*ʿaṣr*), when the largest possible audience had gathered in the mosque. Such sessions at first took place in the Great Mosque of Sidi ʿUqba in Qayrawān, to the great displeasure of the local jurists of the Mālikī *madhhab*. When the new royal city of Manṣūriyya was built to the south of Qayrawān, al-Nuʿmān transferred his sessions to the new Friday mosque in that city, which, like its successor in Cairo, bore the name al-Azhar ('the brilliant' or 'the radiant').[10]

The lessons in the *bāṭin*, or the 'sessions of wisdom' (*majālis al-ḥikma*), on the other hand, were only accessible to initiates. They were held not in the mosque, but within the palace, where admission of the participants was easier to control and where privacy was guaranteed. A special room was reserved for the purpose. Al-Nuʿmān held these sessions in person, as he repeatedly points out. They took place on Fridays, but after the afternoon prayer (*ʿaṣr*), when the crowds had dispersed and only the 'friends of God' (*awliyāʾ Allāh*), as the Ismaili initiates called themselves, had stayed behind.[11]

Everything the *dāʿī* taught in the *majālis al-ḥikma* had to be previously authorized by the imam-caliph himself, for he alone was the repository and dispenser of 'wisdom' (*ḥikma*). Al-Nuʿmān repeatedly mentions that he submitted his lectures in written form for the approval of the caliphs al-Manṣūr (946–953) and al-Muʿizz (953–975). The imam is the source of wisdom, the *dāʿī* is merely his mouthpiece. Al-Nuʿmān describes to us how the *majālis* were organized in the Manṣūriyya palace during the reign of al-Muʿizz:

> When al-Muʿizz li-Dīn Allāh opened the door of compassion to the faithful and turned to them his face full of grace and benevolence, he sent me books of the esoteric knowledge (*ʿilm al-bāṭin*) and ordered me to read them every Friday in a hall (*majlis*) of his palace, as long as he lived. There was a great throng; the room was overcrowded; more people came than could be accommodated. They filled the room he had designated for the assembly, and even a part of the palace's courtyard, so that my voice no longer reached the ones at the very back. This was reported to the imam, and he was informed that among the followers of the *daʿwa*, there were also people who were new and hardly capable of understanding the explanations; these would benefit more if they were separated and assigned a room of their own in which they would be given lectures that they could grasp and understand.

It seems as though al-Nuʿmān himself had made this proposal to the imam, but al-Muʿizz ordered him to continue as before. It did not matter if the whole of the audience was unable to understand everything; each individual would retain from the lectures whatever their mental capacity could grasp, 'just as a pot you put in the rain will catch as much water as will fall into its opening.'[12]

What the Qāḍī al-Nuʿmān taught in his *majālis al-ḥikma* has come down to us in his work 'The Interpretation of the Pillars of Islam' (*Taʾwīl daʿāʾim al-Islām*), the esoteric counterpart to his exoteric compendium of Ismaili law. One represents the *ẓāhir*, the other the *bāṭin*. The 120 chapters of the *Taʾwīl* characteristically bear the title of 'Sessions'.[13]

THREE

The Fatimids in Egypt

On 6 February 969 the Fatimid army under the command of the Slav general, Jawhar, marched from Qayrawān in the direction of Egypt. The caliph al-Muʿizz stayed behind for a while. The seizure of power of the country on the Nile had been carefully prepared. Ismaili missionaries had been active in the Egyptian capital, al-Fusṭāṭ (Old Cairo); Egyptian officials and notables had made secret contacts with the powerful Fatimid caliph. Under the last Ikhshidid emirs, who were nominally governors on behalf of the caliph of Baghdad, Egypt had experienced a major crisis; epidemics and famines had ruined the country and anarchy had crippled its resistance. As the caliph in distant Baghdad could provide no help, the merchants of Egypt in particular placed their hope in the Fatimid caliph, whom they expected to restore public safety, and with it, the prosperity of Egypt.

The Fatimid seizure of power in Egypt was, therefore, carried out peacefully. When Jawhar and his army marched into the Nile Delta in May 969, the notables of al-Fusṭāṭ immediately started negotiations. A delegation led by the supreme judge and the senior representatives of the Ḥasanid and Ḥusaynid descendants of the Prophet, accompanied by the Ismaili *dāʿī* of Old Cairo, negotiated a treaty which assumed the form of a guarantee of safety (*amān*). The Egyptians placed themselves under the protection of the Fatimid caliph, who in turn guaranteed the re-establishment of a stable currency, the safety of the pilgrimage routes and the resumption of the *jihād* against Byzantium. In addition, the maintenance of the *sunna* of the Prophet was ensured. Although in the course of their 200 years of dominion over Egypt, the Fatimids introduced the Ismaili *madhhab* in law and changed certain external aspects of the ritual – such as the call to prayer – in accordance with Ismaili tradition, they never tried forcibly to convert the mass of the Egyptian population, who were and remained Sunni, to the Ismaili creed. The *daʿwa* was limited to the sessions of wisdom (*majālis al-ḥikma*), which no one was compelled to attend.

On 6 July 969, Jawhar's army marched across the bridge which connected Gīza on the left bank of the Nile with al-Fusṭāṭ on the right bank. However, the general did not move into the city of al-Fusṭāṭ; instead he camped a few kilometres to the north-east. In the vicinity of his camp he immediately began to build a new city which was to house the palaces of the Fatimid caliph. This city was first named al-Manṣūriyya, like the royal city near Qayrawān; only later was it re-named al-Qāhira al-Muʿizziyya, 'the Victorious [city] of al-Muʿizz', which we know today as Cairo.

The site of Cairo, a vast square surrounded by a mud-brick wall, was therefore originally not a city properly speaking, but a princely residence to house palaces for the caliph and the crown prince, the treasury, the ministries (*dīwān*) and the army's barracks. South-east of the caliph's palace a mosque was built and named al-Azhar, 'the Radiant One', after its prototype in Manṣūriyya. The Azhar was originally a royal mosque, designed for the caliph and his court. Jawhar's building still forms its core. However, the cluster of buildings that have been added around it in the course of centuries mean that its present external aspect does not provide any idea of the original Fatimid structure. The Azhar was the mosque of the Ismailis, who were not numerous at the time, while the ʿAmr Mosque in the heart of al-Fusṭāṭ (Old Cairo) and the Ibn Ṭūlūn Mosque (between al-Fusṭāṭ and al-Qāhira) were frequented by the Sunnis.

For four years (969–973), General Jawhar ruled Egypt as the Fatimid viceroy and prepared the ground for the transference of the seat of the Fatimid caliphate to Cairo. The Fatimids had no reason to interfere in the complicated administration of Egypt, which had been run by competent officials for centuries. They took into their service almost all the existing officials, even the vizier and the supreme *qāḍī*. However, they attached a Kutāma Berber to each high official as a kind of supervisor. In the summer of 972 preparations for the transfer began in Manṣūriyya/Qayrawān. The entire Fatimid state was, as it were, decamped on camels, donkeys and boats, including the public treasury, which was melted down into bars of gold and silver, and the coffins of the first three caliphs. In November the huge caravan set out, accompanied by the fleet, and in May 973 it arrived in Alexandria where al-Muʿizz received a delegation of Egyptians. On 10 June 973, the imam-caliph rode across the pontoon bridge connecting Gīza with al-Fusṭāṭ and took possession of the palaces built on Jawhar's orders. At his side rode his most faithful follower, al-Qāḍī al-Nuʿmān, the head of the Ismaili *daʿwa*.

The reign of al-Muʿizz in Egypt was destined to be short-lived. The most important event of this period was the victory won by his son al-ʿAzīz, the crown prince elect, in his war against the Qarmaṭīs north of Cairo in May 974. This paved the way for the occupation of Palestine and Syria, which were threatened at this time by a renewed expansion of the Byzantine empire. The Fatimids succeeded in holding Damascus and they acquired the holy cities of Mecca and Medina, which from now on acknowledged the Fatimid caliph as their suzerain.

In both cities of the Ḥijāz it was now the caliph in Cairo, rather than the caliph in Baghdad, for whom blessings were implored at the end of the Friday sermon (*khuṭba*). This acknowledgement at the same time involved an obligation: the Fatimid caliphs were now responsible for the safety and subsistence of pilgrims, and what is more, not only pilgrims from Egypt, but also Andalusians and Maghribīs, Sicilians and Syrians. The wells along the pilgrimage routes had to be kept in repair, food and supplies had to be made available, and a military escort against predatory Bedouins, and above all against the Qarmaṭīs of eastern Arabia, had to be provided. The precious drapery (*kiswa*) with which the Kaʿba was newly decorated each year on the occasion of the *ḥajj* was now woven in Egypt; the *sharīf*s (descendants of the Prophet Muḥammad) in Mecca and Medina received rich pensions from the Fatimid public treasury, and the populations of both holy cities were supplied with Egyptian cereals. The Fatimid imam-caliph had replaced the Abbasid caliph of Baghdad as the protector of the holy sites of Islam.

Al-Muʿizz died in February 975 and was buried in the castle of Cairo. His mausoleum (*turba*), in which other Fatimid caliphs and members of their families were also buried later, was decorated with a splendid wall-hanging which al-Muʿizz had already ordered before his move to Egypt:

> … a magnificent work, on a fine piece of blue silk; it represented the continents with all the cities and mountains, seas and rivers, the entire geography; Mecca and Medina could also be seen on it, and underneath it was written: 'Made on the command of al-Muʿizz li-Dīn Allāh, out of longing for the sanctuary of God, and in order to make known the abodes of the emissary of God, in the year 353 (964)'; 22,000 dinars were spent on it.[1]

The son and successor of al-Muʿizz, al-ʿAzīz bi'llāh, was among the greatest rulers of Islamic history. His reign, which lasted more than twenty years (975–996), was one of the happiest periods in the history of Egypt. The different religious groups among the Egyptian and Syrian populations – Ismailis, Twelver Shiʿis, Sunnis, Christians and Jews – lived together peacefully. At the side of the imam-caliph stood a capable administrator with experience in financial matters, Yaʿqūb ibn Killis, who was appointed vizier in the year 979 and filled this office, with only a brief interruption, until his death in 991. We will presently have more to say about him as patron of the arts and promoter of knowledge.

Direct Fatimid rule covered Egypt, Palestine and southern Syria; indirectly the imam-caliph controlled the Ḥijāz with Mecca and Medina, where local *sharīfs* exercised their power in his name. Similarly, the emirs of Palermo from the house of the Banu'l-Kalb ruled Sicily. They demonstrated their affiliation to the Fatimid empire by means of regular embassies who brought rich presents to Cairo. The whole of the Maghrib was entrusted to viceroys from the Zīrid dynasty, a princely family who belonged to the Berber tribe of the Ṣanhāja (in present-day Algeria) and who, after the departure of the Fatimids, proceeded to occupy the palaces of Manṣūriyya near Qayrawān. They also showed their loyalty towards the imam by regular gifts, and especially by having themselves, just like the emirs of Sicily, initiated into the Ismaili *daʿwa*.

Throughout his reign, time after time, al-ʿAzīz had to take steps to safeguard Palestine and Syria against threats of the Qarmaṭīs, the Byzantines and the rebellious Bedouins. On one occasion the caliph himself took the field in Palestine at the head of his army; when he died in 996 he had just been preparing for another Syrian campaign from a camp near Bilbays in the Nile delta.

The sudden death of al-ʿAzīz led to a critical situation, for the son of the caliph, al-Ḥākim, was only eleven years old. The eunuch Barjawān seized the reins of government, supported by leading military men and officials, but in the year

1000 the young caliph managed to get rid of the regent, who had by then grown far too powerful and highhanded, and assumed authority himself.

The reign of the imam-caliph al-Ḥākim bi-Amr Allāh (996–1021) is one of the most interesting periods of Fatimid history. The image of this ruler has been distorted by subsequent hostile historiography; indeed the anti-Fatimid tradition tried to make a real monster of him. The Christian chronicler, John of Antioch (Yaḥyā al-Anṭākī), offered, from a distance, a diagnosis of mental disorder. Later Sunni authors maintained that he stopped washing himself for seven years, that he lived in an underground room for three years without ever leaving it, and that he worshipped the planets Mars and Saturn. All this is nonsense. Even the reproach that al-Ḥākim was unpredictable and erratic and that he used to countermand instructions he had just given cannot be confirmed from the sources. If we refer to the contemporary annals of Cairo, and above all to al-Ḥākim's edicts (*sijillāt*), as handed down in the sources, we acquire a very different picture.

It is true that the caliph was very suspicious of the officials and dignitaries of his court, and that he severely punished their encroachments and enrichments, their venality and deceit, thus earning himself the reputation of incorruptible justice in the Ismaili sources. This mistrust must have been the result of his unpleasant childhood experiences: from his accession to the throne at the age of eleven until his fifteenth year he was at the mercy of the eunuch Barjawān, who treated him not only as a minor but often as a prisoner. When he finally rid himself of this far too powerful servant, he never again allowed any of his ministers to become all-powerful and always eyed them with distrust. He shared this characteristic with a number of other important rulers in world history, who had suffered from very similar experiences in their youth, such as the German Emperor Frederick II of Hohenstaufen.

Among the people of Cairo the caliph al-Ḥākim was extremely popular. In the early years of his reign he liked to mix with people on both Muslim and Christian holidays, showed himself at night in the narrow lanes of the city's *sūq*s, and gave orders that every petitioner be admitted into his presence. It was also said that he rode out at night in disguise so that he could learn how his subjects felt about his reign. A memory of this nocturnal habit of the Fatimid caliph has been preserved in the tales of the 'Thousand and One Nights' (though it has been attributed to the caliph Hārūn al-Rashīd of Baghdad, about whom the historians say nothing of the kind). In the last years of his life al-Ḥākim displayed an inclination towards asceticism and gave up all pompous display and his splendid retinues. Without a bodyguard, and accompanied only by two grooms, he would modestly ride a donkey, clothed like a Sufi in a simple garment of white wool, with sandals on his feet and his head covered with a cloth in the style of a Bedouin. He evidently had nothing to fear from his subjects. In his last years, however, he found the crowded streets burdensome and preferred to ride out alone at night into the desert or to the mountains east of Cairo, returning in the early hours of the morning while his courtiers awaited him at the city gate.

Contrary to a widespread misconception, al-Ḥākim's religious policy was thoroughly consistent. Until the end he sought to enforce the *sharīʿa* upon his subjects and to urge it under the threat of severe punishment. But he tried to produce a rapprochement between the Sunnis, the Twelver Shiʿis and the Ismailis because he wanted to be the imam of all Muslims. These efforts culminated in May 1009 (Ramaḍān 399) in an edict (*sijill*) of tolerance which legally put Sunni rites on a par with Shiʿi rites. In support of this edict he referred to the well-known Qurʾanic verse II:256: 'No compulsion is there in religion'. The differences between the Islamic confessions remained, but were tolerated. So for instance while the Ismailis counted (*ḥisāb*) the thirty days of Ramaḍān and then broke their fast, the Sunnis ended their month of fasting when the new moon was sighted (*ruʾya*), so that nothing prevented the two confessions from celebrating the feast of breaking the fast (*ʿīd al-fiṭr*) on two different days. The Shiʿa were forbidden the open abuse, on their holidays, of those of the Companions of the Prophet who had opposed ʿAlī, but they were allowed to add the formula 'Arise to the best of deeds!' (*ḥayya ʿalā khayr al-ʿamal*), which was omitted by the Sunni muezzins in the call to prayer (*adhān*). Similarly, when taking an oath, people could use the religious formula of their choice. Al-Ḥākim's *sijill* ended with the liberal principle: 'Each Muslim may try to find his own solution within his religion (*li-kulli Muslim fī dīnihī ijtihād*)'.[2]

Among the Christians, however, al-Ḥākim left bitter memories, for he ordered the destruction of the Church of the Holy Sepulchre in Jerusalem and of a few other churches and convents in Egypt and Sinai. The sources are contradictory on al-Ḥākim's motives, but it seems that these measures were an attempt to contain the rise of anti-Christian sentiment among Muslims who resented their growing wealth and disregard of the *sharīʿa*. However, there was no general persecution of Christians, as has been falsely maintained time and again. There was no edict forcing Christians to convert to Islam although officials, but only officials, were given the choice of converting or emigrating to Byzantine territory. The expropriation of several churches and convents generated much-needed funds for paying the army, a device already often resorted to by earlier Muslim governors or rulers of Egypt. In the last years of his reign, al-Ḥākim returned to the Christians the expropriated churches and convents as well as their lands, and allowed them to reconstruct the demolished buildings. During his rides to the Muqaṭṭam mountains near Cairo, he would even stop for a rest at the Dayr al-Qaṣīr convent, talk with the abbot and inspect the progress of the reconstruction.

Like his father, al-ʿAzīz, al-Ḥākim followed the custom of personally leading the prayer and holding the sermon in one of the four great mosques of Cairo and al-Fusṭāṭ on the four Fridays of Ramaḍān, a tradition also preserved by succeeding Fatimid caliphs. The Friday Mosque which his father had begun to build – the Azhar having become too small – in front of the northern city-gate of Cairo was completed by al-Ḥākim and still bears his name. At the end of the eleventh century, when the city of Cairo was surrounded by a new, larger wall of stone, the Ḥākim Mosque was enclosed in it, so that it is now situated within the wall and behind the 'Gate of Triumphs' (Bāb al-Futūḥ).

The Ḥākim Mosque is the major monument of al-Ḥākim's reign in Cairo. But the imam-caliph also distinguished himself by other activities. He furnished the Azhar Mosque with an entirely new financial basis by granting it a generous endowment (*waqf*). The same is true of the other Friday mosques (*jāmiʿ*) of Cairo, and of the city's numerous small oratories (*masjid*), to which he allocated maintenance funds. His most glorious deed, however, was the founding of a scientific institution, the 'House of Knowledge', which will be discussed later.

From a political point of view the reign of the imam-caliph al-Ḥākim, which lasted a quarter of a century (996–1021), was a period of remarkable stability. An armistice concluded with the emperor of Byzantium in the year 1001 remained in force virtually throughout and was several times renewed. Two attempts at establishing a counter-caliphate failed miserably: an Andalusian adventurer called Abū Rakwa ('the one with the canteen'), who claimed to be an Umayyad prince, tried to conquer Egypt with the help of the Bedouins from Cyrenaica, but was finally defeated by the Fatimid troops and, having taken flight, handed over to al-Ḥākim by the king of Nubia. A similar fiasco was the attempt of the Hāshimid Sharīf of Mecca, Abu'l-Futūḥ al-Ḥasan b. Ja'far, to have himself raised to the Sunni caliphate with the help of the Bedouins of Palestine and Transjordan. Having been abandoned by the Bedouins, the Sharīf of Mecca finally had to recognize once again the suzerainty of the Fatimids.

During the last years of al-Ḥākim's reign there appeared in Cairo certain religious agitators who proclaimed the divinity of al-Ḥākim and the earlier Fatimid caliphs, and declared the commands and prohibitions of the religious law, the *sharī'a*, as null and void. They were what is commonly known as 'exaggerators' (*ghulāt*). This new religious doctrine, which called itself simply 'monotheism' (*dīn al-tawḥīd*), is now known as the Druze religion. Its most famous apostles were Ḥamza al-Labbād ('the felt-maker') and Anūshtikīn al-Darzī (Persian, 'the tailor'). The former laid the foundation for what was to become the sacred scriptures of the Druzes with his epistles (*rasā'il*); the latter lent his name to the sect, as its followers are called 'Darzites' (al-Darziyya) or 'al-Durūz', with a broken Arabic plural. The preaching of these Druze propagandists led to great unrest in Cairo. Al-Darzī was probably executed by the order of al-Ḥākim. Ḥamza managed to escape to Mecca, where the above-mentioned Sharīf Abu'l-Futūḥ, the hapless counter-caliph, had him beheaded.[3]

Later Sunni authors maintained that the Druze leaders were not only tolerated and promoted by al-Ḥākim, but that al-Ḥākim himself had invented and propagated the new doctrine. The Christian chronicler John of Antioch also believed that al-Ḥākim considered himself a prophet, and even as God. This too, like so many other things said about al-Ḥākim by his opponents, is devoid of the slightest evidence. Al-Ḥākim issued a wealth of decrees (*sijillāt*), but among all those mentioned by the chroniclers there is not one in which he claims divinity for himself or proclaims any of the Druze dogmas. The great Ismaili author Ḥamīd al-Dīn al-Kirmānī, the head of the Ismaili mission in Iraq and Iran, was in Cairo at the time and wrote a short work with the title 'The Mouths of the Happy Tidings' (*Mabāsim al-bishārāt*). In it he explained that the imam was only a creature, not the Creator, that he was a servant of God and that a long line of other imams would follow him; in another work, *al-Wāʿiẓa* ('The Warning'), he directly attacked and refuted the central doctrines of the Druze sectarians.[4]

The end of the imam-caliph al-Ḥākim was as remarkable as his entire reign. On the night of 13 February 1021 he failed to return from one of his solitary nocturnal rides. Those who went to search for him found only his donkey with the tendons of its legs cut through, and later his bloodstained garments in a pond. The mystery of his disappearance has never been cleared up. A Berber officer was executed as his alleged murderer. The propaganda of the hostile Baghdad court pointed the finger of suspicion at al-Ḥākim's sister, Sitt al-Mulk, accusing her of having her brother murdered. Later on, a rebel, a Ḥasanid Sharīf, was arrested in Upper Egypt and it is said that shreds of al-Ḥākim's head-covering and even a piece of his scalp were found on him. But all this was dubious. Several false Ḥākims appeared by and by, and for a long time the people hoped, and indeed expected, that the popular caliph and his successful reign might return some day – another characteristic which the Fatimid al-Ḥākim had in common with the Staufer Frederick II.

FOUR

Ismaili Teaching and Learning
ẓāhir and *bāṭin*

It is time and again maintained that the Azhar Mosque was the centre of Ismaili propaganda (*daʿwa*). This is not true, as we shall see. What is true is that, from the very beginning, the Azhar played a major part as an institution of learning. However, it was not primarily the Ismaili esoteric doctrine (*ḥikma*) which was taught here, but Ismaili jurisprudence, hence not what the Ismailis called 'the inner meaning' (*bāṭin*) of the revelation, but 'the external meaning' (*ẓāhir*), the *sharīʿa* according to the Ismaili *madhhab*.

The founder of Ismaili jurisprudence was al-Qāḍī al-Nuʿmān, whom we have already met. When on 10 June 973 the caliph al-Muʿizz made his solemn entry into Cairo, four years after the city's foundation by Jawhar, the Qāḍī al-Nuʿmān was riding at his side. The office of supreme judge was, however, already filled. Jawhar had retained the supreme *qāḍī* Abū Ṭāhir al-Dhuhlī in his position, and al-Muʿizz confirmed the appointment. The contemporary chronicler, Ibn Zūlāq, merely refers to al-Nuʿmān as 'the *dāʿī*',[1] proving that he held the supreme leadership of the *daʿwa* in Cairo as well, although he was now well advanced in age and not able to work for any length of time in Egypt. He died on 27 March 974.

In the early period of the Fatimid caliphate, the supreme

judge (*qāḍī al-quḍāt*) was at the same time the leading missionary (*dāʿī al-duʿāt*); the 'external law' (*ẓāhir*) and its 'inner' meaning (*bāṭin*) were thus entrusted to one and the same person. After the death of the Qāḍī al-Nuʿmān, both functions were reunited first in the hands of his two sons, ʿAlī and Muḥammad, and then in his two grandsons, al-Ḥusayn ibn ʿAlī (999–1004) and ʿAbd al-ʿAzīz ibn Muḥammad (1004–1008).

Al-Qāḍī al-Nuʿmān's sons were both outstanding jurists like their father. On 30 September 976, in the first year of the reign of the caliph al-ʿAzīz (975–996), the elder son, ʿAlī, was solemnly installed to the office of supreme judge:

> Wearing a robe of honour and girt with a sword, he rode to the Azhar Mosque followed by a great suite; in front of him, seventeen splendid robes with turbans were carried. In the mosque, his deed of investiture was read out; he was standing meanwhile, but each time the name of the caliph or of one of his relatives was mentioned, he made a low bow. Then he proceeded to the Old Mosque [the ʿAmr Mosque] in Miṣr [Old Cairo], where the preacher ʿAbd al-Samīʿ was waiting for him. ʿAlī led the Friday prayer; then his brother read out his certificate of appointment. It said that he was assigned the office of judge in Miṣr and its provinces, the office of preacher (*khiṭāba*), the leadership of the prayer (*imāma*) and the supervision over gold and silver, legacies, and weights and measures. Thereupon, he went home … Three days later, ʿAlī ibn al-Nuʿmān rode to the Old Mosque again, with a red casket carried ahead of him; he was accompanied by witnesses, notaries, jurists and merchants. A large crowd of people had assembled. Thus he sat in judgement. He summoned those people who managed the fortunes of others as trustees, recited the 103rd *sūra* to them ['Surely man is in the way of loss, save those who believe, and do righteous deeds, and counsel each other unto the truth …'] and exhorted them to fear God.[2]

The new supreme judge appointed his brother, Muḥammad ibn al-Nuʿmān, to represent him as judge of Tinnīs, Dimyāṭ (Damietta) and Faramā (ancient Pelusium), three cities on the Mediterranean coast of Egypt. In Miṣr (Old Cairo) and Cairo, he administered justice himself on Mondays and Thursdays in the ʿAmr Mosque in Old Cairo, Tuesdays in the royal city of Cairo – probably in the Azhar Mosque – and Saturdays for the courtiers in the caliph's palace. He kept records and documents in his residence; the red casket which was carried ahead of him to his court sessions contained the documents and handbooks needed for the pending cases. It was not until 1015, under the caliph al-Ḥākim, that the judge's records were moved to a special office in the building of the former mint next to the ʿAmr Mosque.

When ʿAlī ibn al-Nuʿmān died on 3 December 984, his brother Muḥammad succeeded him in the office of supreme judge. Like his father and brother, he was not only responsible for justice, but also for the propagation of the Ismaili doctrine, and hence for the *majālis al-ḥikma*. We are told that in April 995 'the Qāḍī Muḥammad ibn al-Nuʿmān was sitting on a seat in the palace, about to read out the sciences of the household of the Prophet (*ʿulūm āl al-bayt*), as he and his brother had already been doing in Egypt and his father in the Maghrib. In the crush eleven people were killed; al-ʿAzīz biʾllāh had them wrapped in shrouds [at his own expense].'[3]

The descendants of the Qāḍī al-Nuʿmān dominated the judicial affairs of the Fatimid empire for many decades. During the reign of the caliph al-ʿAzīz, however, there emerged a competitor in the person of the influential finance officer and subsequent vizier, Yaʿqūb ibn Killis (930–91), a former Jew born in Baghdad who had converted to Islam and had played a decisive part in the Fatimids' assumption of power in Egypt. After the accession of al-ʿAzīz, the forty-nine-year-old Ibn Killis was officially awarded the title of vizier and, except for a brief interruption, conducted the policy of the Fatimid empire for twenty-two years. Ibn Killis himself, assisted by a few jurists, wrote a handbook of Ismaili jurisprudence. This book was based on the sayings of the caliph al-ʿAzīz and the earlier imams and bore the title 'The Viziers' Treatise' (*al-Risāla al-wazīriyya*). It was meant to serve as a handbook and guide for Egyptian jurists, and it was apparently intended to supersede the 'Pillars of Islam' (*Daʿāʾim al-Islām*) of the Qāḍī al-Nuʿmān. As the work has not survived, we do not have any clear idea of its contents. It may possibly have represented a compromise between Ismaili and Sunni laws, but it was not accepted by the Sunni jurists and so the caliph al-ʿAzīz withdrew it from circulation. After that al-Nuʿmān's 'Pillars of Islam' became the undisputed standard work of Ismaili law in the Fatimid empire.

The vizier Ibn Killis was the first to establish a regular teaching centre for law next to the Azhar Mosque. So he was in a sense the founder of the Azhar Mosque as a teaching centre which is famous to this day:

> In the year 378 [of the Hijra, i.e., 988], the vizier Abu'l-Faraj Yaʿqūb ibn Yūsuf ibn Killis asked the caliph al-ʿAzīz bi'llāh to specify the salaries for a few jurists. Thereupon, the caliph granted each of them a sufficient salary. He ordered a piece of land to be bought and a house to be built next to the Azhar Mosque. Each Friday they assembled in the mosque and formed circles after the [mid-day] prayer until the time for the afternoon prayer (*ʿaṣr*). They also received a certain sum each year out of the vizier's own fortune. Their number was thirty-five; on the feast of breaking the fast (*fiṭr*), al-ʿAzīz presented them with robes of honour and let them ride through the city on mules.[4]

This arrangement could hardly be called a 'university'; it merely consisted of holding public lectures on law according to the Ismaili *madhhab* with the jurists receiving a salary out of the private purse of the caliph or the vizier. There was not even an endowment (*waqf*), which would have lent permanence to the institution. This meant that the teaching centre at the Azhar Mosque probably only existed during the lifetimes of the vizier Ibn Killis (d. 991) and the caliph al-ʿAzīz (d. 996). As we shall see below, it was al-ʿAzīz's son and successor, al-Ḥākim, who established this teaching centre on an entirely new basis.

We have already pointed out that access to the sessions of legal instruction and hence to the *ẓāhir* was open to everyone. It was the aim of the Fatimid caliphs to have the 'law of the house of the Prophet', i.e., the Ismaili *madhhab*, gradually become the established school of law within the empire. Public lectures on Ismaili law (*fiqh*) were, therefore, provided in the mosque, and were accessible to all. As we have seen, these had been held in the Azhar Mosque since the year 988 by the thirty-five jurists in the service of the caliph and his vizier. The supreme *qāḍī* al-Ḥusayn ibn ʿAlī ibn al-Nuʿmān is even reported to have given lectures on jurisprudence in the 'Old Mosque', i.e., the ʿAmr Mosque in al-Fusṭāṭ, which was the principal mosque of the Sunnis.[5] The sons and grandsons of the Qāḍī al-Nuʿmān based themselves on the latter's major work, the 'Pillars of Islam' (*Daʿāʾim al-Islām*) and the 'Abridged Version' (*al-Iqtiṣār*) of his *al-Īḍāḥ*, as well as other books that are used by the Ismailis to this day.[6]

These purely legal lectures in the ʿAmr and the Azhar Mosques were quite different from the 'sessions of wisdom' (*majālis al-ḥikma*), which were open exclusively to initiates who had already taken the oath of allegiance (*ʿahd*) to the imam. For more efficient control over the access to these sessions, they were held inside the caliph's palace.

A description of these sessions is provided by al-Musabbiḥī, the close friend and court chronicler of the caliph al-Ḥākim:

> The *dāʿī* used to hold continuous sessions in the palace to read what was read to the saintly [*al-awliyāʾ* = the intiates] and [collect] the dues connected with it. [The *dāʿī*] would hold a separate session for the *awliyāʾ*; another for the courtiers (*al-khāṣṣa*) and high officials as well as all those attached to the palaces as servants or in other capacities; a further session for the simple people and strangers in the city; a separate session for women in the Mosque of Qāhira called al-Azhar; and a session for the wives (*ḥurum, scil.* of the caliph) and the noble women of the palaces. He wrote the *majālis* at home and then sent them to the person in charge of serving the state. For

> these *majālis* he used books, of which fair copies were made after they were submitted to the caliph. At each of these sessions he collected the *najwā* which was taken in gold and silver from all men and women who paid a part of it, and he noted the names of those who had paid; he equally noted, on the feast of breaking the fast (*fiṭr*), how much *fiṭra* had been paid. This amounted to a handsome sum which he each time delivered to the state purse (*bayt al-māl*). The sessions of the mission were called Sessions of Wisdom (*majālis al-ḥikma*).[7]

This text gives us some interesting information. We learn that there were several different types of teaching sessions, some of which were evidently public and would certainly not give away the esoteric aspects of the doctrine. Thus, we can hardly imagine that the 'simple people and strangers in the city' were admitted to the actual *majālis al-ḥikma*; it is more likely that these were elementary sessions to arouse the curiosity of the non-initiate. The Azhar Mosque as a place for these lectures only appears marginally: here introductory courses were held for women, which were no doubt public as well.

The text further confirms what we already know about the Qāḍī al-Nuʿmān's *majālis al-ḥikma* in Ifrīqiya: that the *dāʿī* had to have his manuscripts personally authorized by the imam-caliph. The imam was the real source of wisdom (*ḥikma*) and the *dāʿī* merely his mouthpiece. The drafts for the lectures were probably prepared by the *dāʿī*, but they were then submitted to the imam, who would approve or perhaps correct them. Only thus was the authenticity and purity of the doctrine guaranteed.

The teaching sessions for the initiates did not merely serve to instruct them. Our text reports that on these occasions the believers also had to pay certain dues, the *najwā* and the *fiṭra*. The term *najwā* means 'confidential discussion' and probably refers to the Qur'an (LVIII:12): 'Ye faithful! If you have something confidential to discuss (*najaytum*) with the Envoy, then prior to your confidential discussion (*najwākum*) pay some alms (*ṣadaqa*) in anticipation.' So, according to Ismaili doctrine, the instructions in the *majālis al-ḥikma* corresponded to the erstwhile conversations with the Prophet himself. The *najwā* is a charitable gift which the believer makes to show his gratitude for the favour of the instruction. The other gift, the *fiṭra*, was to be made on the day of the feast of breaking the fast (*ʿīd al-fiṭr*) after the end of the month of Ramaḍān; it was acknowledged by the imam by way of a sweet pastry which was distributed on that holiday to all believers – courtiers, officials, guardsmen and servants – in the great hall of the palace (*al-īwān al-kabīr*). As the number of Ismaili followers rapidly increased at the court of Cairo, the palace kitchens were no longer in a position to supply the large quantities of pastries required. The caliph al-ʿAzīz, therefore, found it necessary to organize a special place, the *dār al-fiṭra*, which was situated close by the palace. The production of the *fiṭra* pastry cost 10,000 gold dinars a year. The recipe has come down to us:[8] 1,000 loads of flour, 700 quintals of sugar, 6 quintals of pistachios, 8 quintals of walnuts, 4 quintals of hazelnuts, 400 *irdabb* of dates (1 *irdabb* = 198 litres), 300 *irdabb* of raisins, 5 quintals of honey, 200 quintals of sesame oil, two *irdabb* each of sesame seed and aniseed; in addition, there were the expenses for firewood and lamp oil, musk, camphor and saffron, as well as the wages for the bakers.

Apart from al-Musabbiḥī's text quoted above there are a few other sources about the *majālis al-ḥikma*. There is, first of all, a non-dated document (*sijill*) about the appointment of an unnamed *dāʿī*, the text of which has come down to us in the handbook of officials of al-Qalqashandī.[9] In it the future *dāʿī* is instructed as follows: 'Read the *majālis al-ḥikam*, which were handed to you at the court, to the faithful [i.e., the Ismailis], male and female, and to the adepts, male and female, in the brilliant palaces of the caliphs and in the Friday mosque in al-Muʿizziyya al-Qāhira (the Azhar Mosque of Cairo). But keep the secrets of the wisdom from the unauthorized, and distribute them only to those who are entitled to them! Do not reveal to the weak what they are unable to grasp, but at the same time, do not look upon their understanding as too poor to absorb it!'

This anonymous decree is confirmed by another from the year 1004 – that is from the reign of al-Ḥākim – in which the supreme *qāḍī* ʿAbd al-ʿAzīz ibn Muḥammad ibn al-Nuʿmān delegates the *majālis al-ḥikma* to a deputy:[10] 'He issued a *sijill* for him, authorizing him to collect the *fiṭra* and the *najwā*, to appear in the session room (*majlis*) in the palace, to initiate people,[11] and to lecture to those who had joined the *daʿwa*. Thus he appeared on Thursday 12 [Ramaḍān 394/July 1004], held the usual lecture in the palace, and collected the *najwā* and the *fiṭra*.'

The fourth and last important source stems from a chronicler of the late Fatimid period, Ibn al-Ṭuwayr (1130–1220):

> The *dāʿī al-duʿāt* immediately follows the *qāḍī al-quḍāt* in rank and wears the same attire and other insignia. He has to know the entire jurisprudence of the holy family (*madhāhib āl al-bayt*) and hold lectures about it; he must administer the oath (*ʿahd*) to anyone converting from his own *madhhab* to their *madhhab*. He has twelve stewards (*nuqabāʾ*) of the faithful under his command; in addition, he has deputies (*nuwwāb*) in all cities like deputy judges. The jurists of the dynasty (*fuqahāʾ al-dawla*) appear before him; they have a place called Dār al-ʿIlm, and some of them receive substantial salaries because of their superior positions in it. The jurists among them usually administer the *fatwā* on the strength of a booklet (*daftar*) called *majlis al-ḥikma*, which is read out every Monday and Thursday. It is presented to the supreme *dāʿī* in a fair copy; he hands it to them and takes it back from them. On the two days referred to, he brings it to the caliph and reads it to him, if possible, and receives his signature (*ʿalāma*) on the back of it. He holds sessions in the palace to read it out to the faithful, and he does this at two different places: for the men on the pulpit of the mission (*kursī al-daʿwa*) in the great hall (*al-īwān al-kabīr*), and for the women in the room (*majlis*) of the *dāʿī*, one of the largest and most spacious buildings [in the palace].
>
> When he has finished the reading in front of the faithful men and women, they walk up to him and kiss his hands, and he touches

their heads with the place of the signature, that is the monogram (*khaṭṭ*) of the caliph. He also collects the *najwā* from the faithful of Cairo, Miṣr [al-Fusṭāṭ] and the provinces belonging to it, especially upper Egypt; it amounts [per head] to three and a third dirhams. This adds up to a considerable sum; he presents this to the caliph and hands it to him in private, whereby only God alone is the guarantor [for the completeness of the sum]. Thereupon, the caliph determines a certain amount for him and his stewards. There are some well-to-do Ismailis who pay thirty-three and two-third dinars as *najwā*; together with it, they deliver a piece of paper on which their name is written; this is separated from the petitions and then given back to them with a note written in the caliph's own hand: 'God bless you, your fortune, your descendants and your faith'. This [autograph] is proudly kept [by the contributor]. This service was handed down from father to son in a family called Banū ʿAbd al-Qawī, whose last member was al-Jālis. [The vizier] al-Afḍal [reigned 1094–1121] had exiled them into the Maghrib, so that al-Jālis was born and bred there and inclined towards the *madhhab* of the Sunnis. [Later, in Egypt] he assumed the office of the *qāḍī* and the *daʿwa*. Asad al-Dīn Shīrkūh still lived to see him, highly esteemed him and made him vizier with the caliph al-ʿĀḍid [1160–1171]. He blocked the access to al-ʿĀḍid; otherwise there would have remained nothing in the treasuries because of his generosity, as though he knew that he would be the last [Fatimid] caliph.[12]

So far we have discussed teachers and teaching sessions at great length, without going into any details about the content of the Ismaili *daʿwa* or about the substance of its 'wisdom' (*ḥikma*).

We have already mentioned that, according to the Ismaili conception, there is, in the exoteric (*ẓāhir*) wording of the Qurʾan and the commandments and prohibitions of the *sharīʿa*, an inherent esoteric (*bāṭin*) meaning. This is the essential core of the divine revelation; its truth stems from God and is therefore eternal and immutable.

The earlier religions replaced by Islam all contained the same core of eternal truth only they were clothed in a different form of outward prescriptions and laws. Several revelations of religious laws thus followed one another, each proclaimed by a prophet who, in the terminology of the Ismailis, was called 'the speaker' (*al-nāṭiq*). Adam, Noah, Abraham, Moses, Jesus and Muḥammad are the six speaker-prophets who have announced the six successive religious laws. The Islamic *sharīʿa* is the latest and last of them, and will be valid to the end of time.

Beside each of the 'speakers', however, stands an assistant who has the specific task of preserving and transmitting the 'inner meaning' (*bāṭin*). In the linguistic usage of the Ismailis, he is called the 'legatee' (*waṣī*) or the 'foundation' (*asās*): Abel, Shem, Ishmael, Aaron, Simon Peter and ʿAlī ibn Abī Ṭālib. Each of them is followed by a number of imams who hand down the 'wisdom' from generation to generation, leading and guiding the community of the faithful (*muʾminūn*).

This earliest form of the Ismaili doctrine is known to us only in rough outline, since the sources are very incomplete. We are much better acquainted with the form in which the doctrine asserted itself from the tenth century onwards and was authorized by the imam-caliphs of Cairo. At this time, Ismaili theology was undergoing a significant evolution, one comparable to the development of Christian theology 300 years later, at the time of the great theologian St Thomas Aquinas. It was indeed considerably in advance of the Christian Occident that the Islamic world came to know translations of the works of Greek thinkers and philosophers, and hence to absorb Aristotelian, Platonic and Neoplatonic traditions; and just as the Christian scholastics re-formulated Christian dogmas in the light of Greek philosophy, without changing them in their substance, so the Ismaili theologians also reworded their religious tradition in the then most modern philosophical terminology, without interfering with the essence of the traditional message. This modernization of the message was thoroughly in keeping with the fundamental conviction of the

Ismailis that the eternal divine revelation always remains one and the same, even when couched in different 'exoteric' wordings.

One of the earliest non-Ismaili witnesses of this new development in Ismaili theology was the Sunni theologian al-Māturīdī, who died in Samarkand in 944 AD. He already knew the Ismaili doctrine in its new philosophical terminology. A younger witness, also from Transoxiana, was the famous physician and philosopher Ibn Sīnā, known in the West as Avicenna (980–1037). In his autobiography, Avicenna, who grew up in Bukhara, says: 'My father was one of the Ismailis. He and my brother had accepted their special doctrine of the Soul and the Intellect. They sometimes talked about it while I was listening. I understood what they were saying, but did not agree with them.'

'Soul' (*nafs*) and 'intellect' (*ʿaql*) are two of the crucial concepts of Ismaili theology as we know it today from several original Ismaili writings. One of the first authors whose philosophical–theological system has come down to us – albeit in fragmentary form and in rough outline – is Muḥammad al-Nakhshabī (or al-Nasafi), who operated as a *dāʿī* in Marw al-Rūdh (nowadays northern Afghanistan) and Bukhara, where he was executed in the year 943, a victim of anti-Ismaili persecution. Al-Nakhshabī was the author of a work entitled 'The Book of the Yield' (*Kitāb al-Maḥṣūl*) which has not survived in its original version but, judging by the numerous quotations from it by later authors, must have enjoyed a wide distribution and readership. A later critic has summarized its content as follows:

> While man has sprung from sentient creatures [i.e. animals], these have sprung from vegetal beings [plants], and these in their turn from combined substances, these from elementary qualities, these from celestial bodies, these from the [universal] soul, this from the [universal] intellect, [and] the intellect, however, from the command

> [of the Creator], whereby the command is merely an effect of the Creator, just as light arises from luminosity and the imprint on sealing-wax from the seal ... When the command [of creation] calls forth the intellect – this is what they consider the first, for the command itself is not counted, although it exists prior to the intellect and is a kind of intermediacy between the Creator and the intellect – and the intellect then calls forth the second, namely the soul, then the soul moves, and through its movement the celestial bodies move, while the soul moves within them, and the celestial bodies bring forth the elementary qualities, that is heat, cold, humidity and dryness. These fall among the celestial bodies which revolve around them. They collect in the centre, which assumes the form of a sphere. Cold and dryness combine in the centre and find their place there; humidity rises upwards in search of its place, and combined with the cold it surrounds the earth [as an envelope of water]. Then heat rises from the water and combines with humidity; air emerges and envelops water and earth. Then heat separates from both, is reflected and combines a little with earth; thus a sphere is formed which surrounds the air ... That is fire, but they [the Ismailis] call it ether. When the spheres then revolve and the elementary qualities and combined substances mix, plants are formed; these are purified, and from their quintessence sentient animals come into being. These are purified in their turn, and from them there emerge rational beings. That is the last link of the chain.[13]

These cosmological speculations, which were extremely modern in those days and at the peak of contemporary thought, were easy to combine with the traditional religious doctrines of the Ismailis. In the above text, the process of creation from the origin of the universal intellect down to the genesis of man is described as a *descending* scale; as a counterpart, the Ismaili doctrine propounded an *ascending* scale, the progression of the individual human soul on its way back and upward towards its creator. The Ismaili doctrine of salvation (soteriology) thus forms the necessary counterpart to the theory of the origin of the universe (cosmology).

It is not surprising that such speculations, carried on at a very high intellectual level and couched in the most modern philosophical terminology, were highly attractive to the intellectuals of the Islamic world. The Ismaili mission (*daʿwa*) had proved successful not only among highlanders, peasants and nomads, but equally among the middle classes of large cities.

Of course, the details of these speculations in the new philosophical language led to heated debates. Al-Nakhshabī's book *al-Maḥṣūl* was criticized by another Ismaili *dāʿī*, Abū Ḥātim al-Rāzī (d. 934), who was operating in Rayy (near present-day Tehran), and whose work 'The Book of Correction' (*Kitāb al-Iṣlāḥ*) is still extant. Al-Rāzī was apparently a Qarmaṭī. As regards the official point of view of the Fatimid *daʿwa*, it is known to us from the 'Book of the Support' (*Kitāb al-Nuṣra*) of Abū Yaʿqūb al-Sijistānī (died between 996 and 1003), who was active in central and eastern Iran as a missionary of the imam-caliphs, and of whom a number of writings in the Arabic and Persian languages have survived. Thanks to recent studies by Paul E. Walker, we are quite familiar with his philosophico-theological system.[14]

The eleventh century marked the climax of literary activity among Ismaili authors of the Fatimid period. The man who completed the philosophico-theological system of the *daʿwa* was Ḥamīd al-Dīn al-Kirmānī. He worked mainly in Iraq and Iran, but from 1015 spent a number of years at the court of the imam-caliph, al-Ḥākim, in Cairo where he distinguished himself by guarding against the emerging teachings of the Druzes. Al-Kirmānī had the last word in the controversy among his predecessors al-Nakhshabī, al-Rāzī, and al-Sijistānī by clarifying the points at issue in a special work (*Kitāb al-riyāḍ*). In the year 1020, he also for the first time systematically expounded the whole of the now completed system of the doctrine in a voluminous book, the 'Peace of the Intellect' (*Rāḥat al-ʿaql*). This work, which is one of the greatest achievements of Ismaili thought, shows al-Kirmānī's familiarity not only with Aristotelian and Neoplatonic philosophy, but also with the more recent metaphysical systems of authors like al-Kindī, al-Fārābī and Ibn Sīnā (Avicenna). The 'Peace of the Intellect' has been edited twice and has recently, in 1995, been disclosed in all its depth in a comprehensive study by the Belgian scholar Daniel De Smet.[15]

The *dāʿī* al-Muʾayyad fi'l-Dīn al-Shīrāzī (ca. 1000–1078), who operated in western Iran and Iraq under the Fatimid caliph al-Mustanṣir (1036–1094), has left an autobiography (*al-Sīra*) that gives us an insight into the missionary as well as political activity of a *dāʿī* in those days. In the year 1047 he travelled to Cairo, as was the custom, and came into contact with the supreme *dāʿī* al-Qāsim ibn ʿAbd al-ʿAzīz, a great-grandson of the Qāḍī al-Nuʿmān, and subsequently also with the imam-caliph himself. A few years later, in 1058, al-Muʾayyad himself was raised to the rank of supreme *dāʿī* and held the teaching sessions (*majālis al-ḥikma*) in Cairo. The written version of these, *al-Majālis al-Muʾayyadiyya* – eight volumes containing a hundred 'sessions' each – belongs to the most significant achievements of Ismaili theological-philosophical literature.

A contemporary of al-Muʾayyad's was Nāṣir ibn Khusraw (Persian, Nāṣir-i Khusraw) Qubādiyānī, who was born in 1004 in Qubādiyān near Balkh. He was the son of an official, and himself took up the career of a scribe (*kātib*). In Marw (today's Mary in Turkmenistan), the capital of the province of Khorasan, he was active for a while as an official in the financial administration, but soon after his fortieth year he went through a personal crisis and decided to change his former way of life and go on a pilgrimage to Mecca. In 1046 he left home and set off on a journey that was to continue for seven years. In 1047, in the same year as al-Muʾayyad, he went to Cairo to the court of the imam-caliph al-Mustanṣir, where he remained for three years. It appears that within this time he received intensive training as an Ismaili *dāʿī*; al-Muʾayyad al-Shīrāzī, of whom he later preserved a fond memory, must have played a decisive role in this respect. In his 'Travelogue' (*Safar-nāma*), Nāṣir-i Khusraw provides a detailed description of the city of Cairo, its palaces and its daily life, which is numbered among the major sources for the history of the Fatimid caliphate in this period.

In 1050 Nāṣir-i Khusraw left Cairo and travelled via the Ḥijāz, the Persian Gulf region, Iraq and Iran back to his native country, where he arrived in 1052. He settled in Balkh (ancient Bactra, near today's Mazār-i Sharīf in northern Afghanistan) and thence launched into an extensive missionary activity in the regions between the Caspian Sea and the Hindukush. The hostility of the Sunni *ʿulamāʾ*, who denounced him as a heretic, destroyed his house and threatened his life, finally forced him around 1060 to leave Balkh and to settle down further east in the region of Badakhshān, in the Yumgān valley on the river Kokcha (a southern tributary of the Oxus/Amū Daryā), where he lived until his death (ca. 1090). It was here in exile that most of his works were written, all of them in the Persian language: the already mentioned 'Travelogue' (*Safar-nāma*), which has been translated into several European languages, his *Dīwān* – showing that he is to be counted among the major poets of the Persian language – as well as his philosophico-theological writings, among which the 'Travellers' Provisions' (*Zād al-musāfirīn*) of the year 1061 and the 'Book Joining the Two Wisdoms' (*Kitāb jāmiʿ al-ḥikmatayn*) of the year 1070 deserve particular mention. Nāṣir-i Khusraw was the founder of the Ismaili communities that still exist in Afghan Badakhshān, and in the Badakhshān province of Tajikistan in Central Asia, whose offshoots are the Ismaili communities in Hunza in northern Pakistan. The Ismailis of these regions revere Nāṣir-i Khusraw under the name of Pīr or Shāh Sayyid Nāṣir; his mausoleum, called Ḥaḍrat-i Sayyid, can still be seen on a hill in the vicinity of the village of Jurm near Fayḍābād in north-eastern Afghanistan.

FIVE

The Organization of the *Daʿwa*

The Ismaili mission or 'summons' (*al-daʿwa*) had a strictly hierarchical structure. At its head was the imam, that is the Fatimid caliph who, as a descendant and heir of the Prophet Muḥammad, was the true repository of knowledge or wisdom (*ḥikma*). It was in his name and on his behalf that the chief *dāʿī* (*dāʿī al-duʿāt*) carried out his activities. In the contemporary Ismaili sources the latter is often referred to as 'the gate' (*al-bāb*), as it was only through him that the follower could attain wisdom. We have already seen that in Fatimid Cairo the chief *dāʿī* was also, in most cases, the supreme judge (*qāḍī al-quḍāt*), so that both the 'exoteric' (*ẓāhir*) form of the law, the *sharīʿa*, and its 'esoteric' meaning (*bāṭin*) were entrusted to the care of one and the same person. The chief *dāʿī* prepared the 'sessions of wisdom' (*majālis al-ḥikma*) by personally writing out the texts of the weekly lectures, submitting them to the imam for his examination and, if necessary, correction, and having them authorized by his signature. The texts of the lectures were collected, and it is highly probable that copies of them were sent to the *dāʿīs* all over the Muslim world to ensure that the doctrine was uniformly taught in all Ismaili communities in accordance with the imam's views. It is thanks to this circumstance that the *majālis* of various imams and their chief *dāʿīs* have come down to us in numerous manuscripts.

Within the borders of the Fatimid empire there must also have existed *dāʿīs*, at least in the larger cities, who recruited neophytes, administered the oath to them and subsequently instructed them in their sessions. Unfortunately, we do not know much about such an organization since our sources do not refer to it. The *daʿwa* organization in the Fatimid empire must have been something so commonplace and familiar that the chroniclers did not find it necessary to mention it. So it is by pure chance that we occasionally obtain a piece of information. We thus learn that in the former royal city of the Fatimids in Manṣūriyya near Qayrawān (in what is now Tunisia) there was a 'House of the Ismailis' (*dār al-Ismāʿīliyya*) which was probably responsible for the entire mission in the Maghrib, and no doubt also in Sicily and al-Andalus (today's Spain and Portugal). Such mission centres must also have existed in other parts of the empire. We know, for example, that the cities of Ascalon, Ramla and Akkon in Palestine, Tyre in present-day Lebanon and Jabal al-Summāq (today's Jabal al-Zāwiya near Ḥamāh) in Syria were centres of the Ismaili mission. This is reported by the Qāḍī ʿAbd al-Jabbār in his comprehensive account of the Ismailis.

About the *daʿwa* outside the borders of the Fatimid sphere of influence, we should normally have much less information since the activity of the *dāʿīs* in such places was for the most part carried out clandestinely. Nevertheless, both the Ismaili sources and the non-Ismaili chronicles of the period in fact contain quite a lot of scattered details which can be pieced together, like a puzzle, to produce a reasonably clear picture of the *daʿwa*, if only in outline.

The *daʿwa* outside the empire was organized in 'islands' (*jazāʾir*, singular *jazīra*) under the control of a higher-ranking *dāʿī* who bore the title of *ḥujja* (argument, proof or guarantor). The number of such 'islands' is always stated as twelve in the Ismaili writings, but this number is no doubt meant to be symbolic; it refers to 'the whole' or 'the totality'. In fact, the contemporary sources do not provide evidence for so many 'islands'.

The famous *dāʿī* Ḥamīd al-Dīn al-Kirmānī refers to himself at the beginning of his book 'The Peace of the Intellect' (*Rāḥat al-ʿaql*), as '*dāʿī* of the island of Iraq' (*al-dāʿī bi-jazīrat al-ʿIrāq*). Since the title of one of his other works is 'The Baṣra and Baghdad Sessions', we may conclude that Baghdad and Baṣra were his major centres of activity. A second island was the Yemen, and a third Sind, which was connected with Cairo via Aden in the Yemen. The entire Iranian plateau and Transoxiana were covered by a network of Ismaili communities, but we have no precise information about their internal organization. Shīrāz in the province of Fārs was the centre of operations of the distinguished *dāʿī* al-Mu'ayyad, who was probably in charge of the entire south-western part of Iran. In the north-west was Rayy (south of present-day Tehran), the most important city of the Jibāl province since antiquity, and a major centre of the *daʿwa* from its very beginnings whence it also supervised the communities in the highlands of Daylam south of the Caspian Sea. In north-eastern Iran the province of Khorasan must have been an 'island' in itself, although it appears temporarily – for example under al-Sijistānī and under Nāṣir-i Khusraw – to have been united in the same hands as that of Rayy.

Subordinate to the *ḥujja* were numerous regional and local *dāʿī*s who, in their turn, had several assistants or *ma'dhūn*, literally, deputy. The lowest rank of the hierarchy was filled by the *mukāsir* (breaker), a term derived from the Arabic verb *kasara*, formed by analogy with *munāẓir* (disputant). The *mukāsir* had the task of 'working on' the pupil and disputing with him until all his arguments were refuted. In al-Naysābūrī's instructions for the work of the *dāʿī*s, which will be discussed below, the author says that the recruiter 'should start by breaking the resistance [of the pupil] and destroying his former opinions; he should break his conviction until he has no counter-arguments left.'

The individual *dāʿī* was responsible for a certain district through which he had to make regular inspection tours. The same was true of the *ḥujja* on the higher level of the 'island'. The *ḥujja* must also have been responsible for the training and appointment of his *dāʿī*s; but it seems to have been the rule that all *dāʿī*s, or at least those with a higher rank, were, if feasible, sent to Cairo for a certain time to meet the chief *dāʿī* personally, and possibly the imam, and to be schooled at the centre of the movement. The Iranian *dāʿī*s al-Kirmānī, al-Mu'ayyad al-Shīrāzī, Nāṣir-i Khusraw, and Ḥasan-i Ṣabbāḥ all spent several years in Cairo.

Ḥasan-i Ṣabbāḥ, who was to become master of the Alamūt fortress, may serve as an example for the career of a *dāʿī*. His background is well-known to us thanks to his autobiography entitled 'The Biography of our Lord' (*Sargudhasht-i Sayyidnā*), which the Mongols found in the library of the fortress after capturing Alamūt in 1256, and from which several long quotations by contemporary chroniclers have survived.

Ḥasan-i Ṣabbāḥ was born in Qum. He was originally a Twelver Shīʿi (*Ithnā-ʿasharī*) like his father. But when his father moved to Rayy, Ḥasan soon came into contact with the very ancient and very active local Ismaili community. As with Nāṣir-i Khusraw, it appears to have been a personal crisis – in this case a grave illness – which motivated him to renounce his previous confession and turn towards the Ismailis. Ḥasan-i Ṣabbāḥ was recruited and initiated by several *dāʿī*s and took the oath in 1071. After long years of training and travelling in Iṣfahān, Azerbaijan and Iraq, he went via Damascus and Beirut to Cairo, where he arrived in 1078 and stayed for three years. The year 1081 found him back in Iṣfahān, and during the following nine years he travelled all over Iran spreading the faith as a *dāʿī*, above all in the Daylam highlands south of the Caspian Sea. Here he finally carried off his most spectacular coup in the year 1090: the capture of the Alamūt fortress, which he never left until his death in 1124, and which, in the year 1094 – after the schism that followed the caliph al-Mustanṣir's succession dispute and the murder of the Imam Nizār in Cairo – became the centre of the Nizārī branch of the *daʿwa*.

With the centre of the *daʿwa* in Cairo, the *ḥujjas* and *dāʿīs* communicated through couriers, who took to the imam the contributions of the members of the different 'islands' – as long as they were not needed in the 'island' itself – and on their way home from Cairo, brought back the imam's instructions and letters, and probably certain books reflecting the latest state of the doctrine. These couriers travelled for the most part under an inconspicuous cover, as merchants or pilgrims or using some other disguise. They could, for example, travel as pilgrims to Mecca, say from Sind by boat to Aden and from there with the Yemeni pilgrim caravan to Mecca. Once the *ḥajj* was over they could go on to Cairo with the caravan of the pilgrims returning to Egypt and the Maghrib, without making themselves conspicuous. This was how the Cairo centre always stayed in close touch even with the most remote 'islands' and had detailed information about everything that happened in them.

On the training of the *dāʿīs* we have no precise information. There are, however, two texts from the Fatimid period which deal at length with the virtues of the *dāʿī* and the qualities he required to carry out his mission, providing us, as it were, with a picture of the ideal *dāʿī*. Both texts belong to the genre of literature that was called *adab* (appropriate behaviour, good manners) in Arabic which also exists for other professions: the appropriate behaviour of the scribe or state secretary (*adab al-kātib*) or of the judge (*adab al-qāḍī*); here we are dealing with the genre *adab al-dāʿī*.

The author of the first of these two texts is the Qāḍī al-Nuʿmān; its title is 'The Book of Devotion: The Good Manners of the Followers of the Imam' (*Kitāb al-himma fi ādāb atbāʿ al-aʾimma*). In this short book al-Nuʿmān impresses upon all believers (*muʾminūn*), that is all Ismailis, fitting conduct towards the imam and above all in the presence of the imam. The last chapter is entitled: 'How those who carry out missions for the imam are to conduct themselves'. It is a text of only four pages, but it includes all the principles of the Ismaili learning tradition.

The summons (*daʿwa*) teaching is a divine task, for God said to his envoy Muḥammad: 'Call to the way of your Lord with wisdom and good exhortation' (Qurʾan XVI: 125). To elucidate this word of God, al-Nuʿmān quotes maxims that are – as might be expected – sayings of the imams, especially of that particular imam who had always been considered the most learned of them all, Jaʿfar al-Ṣādiq, whom the Ismailis count as the fifth imam while the Twelver Shiʿi consider him as the sixth.

Imam Jaʿfar said: 'Study in order to acquire learning, and to adorn yourself with it; cultivate dignity and goodwill; treat with respect those who teach you, and those whom you teach. Do not make your learning oppressive to anyone, and do not permit your vanity to destroy the effects of what is really good in you.' He also said: 'Those who acquire learning merely for the purpose of opposing the learned, or teasing fools, or attracting the attention of the public and of showing their own superiority over others, such people shall be punished after death, because [religious] leadership should belong only to those who really deserve it.'

Learning, according to the Qāḍī al-Nuʿmān, is all too often motivated by ambition, by the desire to surpass others and have reason to boast in front of others. Rivalry with friends and colleagues plays an important part in this respect. The major aim of the ambitious man is to attain high status. Such ambition is not, however, necessarily harmful. Indeed as an initial driving force, a first impulse, it is even useful; but that should not be all, for not until the learner delves into the spirit of his activity is his learning really crowned with success. Al-Nuʿmān quotes someone who rightly said: 'By God! At first we do not study to acquire learning for the sake of God; but gradually knowledge which we acquire works upon us in such a way that we ultimately turn to Him.' 'Be silent *dāʿī*s for us,' Imam Jaʿfar bids his followers, meaning: behave in such a way that your example alone be sufficient proof of the superiority of your religion.

Besides the short chapter in the Qāḍī al-Nuʿmān's *al-Himma*, there exists a much more comprehensive treatise of the genre *adab al-dāʿī* from the pen of the *dāʿī* Aḥmad al-Naysābūrī, who operated under the Imams al-ʿAzīz and al-Ḥākim. His treatise, a kind of manual of the ideal *dāʿī*, is entitled 'A Brief Epistle on the Requisites of the Rightly-guiding Mission' (*al-Risāla al-mūjaza fī shurūṭ al-daʿwa al-hādiya*). In this writing we again come across the same image of learning as a kind of rebirth as was used in the initiation romance 'The Teacher and the Pupil': just as the husband engenders a son, but no longer intervenes in the development of the embryo in the womb, only looking after the mother instead, so the imam 'engenders' knowledge in the *dāʿī*, his pupil, and continues to care for the well-being of the *dāʿī* – his spouse, as it were – but leaves the growth and ripening of the knowledge, the embryo, to itself.

Al-Naysābūrī's treatise in fact grants the *dāʿī* a relatively high measure of autonomy and makes correspondingly high demands on him. It may be assumed that the treatise here truly reflects the reality of the Fatimid *daʿwa*. The *dāʿī*s often operated in countries far away from Cairo, in Sind, Badakhshān (Afghanistan and Tajikistan) or Transoxiana (Uzbekistan); liaisons with the centre were slow and difficult, couriers and letters were often en route for months. In addition there was the often hostile environment, complicating or completely preventing an open appearance of the *dāʿīs*. There were admittedly occasions when the *dāʿī* was able to secure the protection of a local ruler. Thus, the *dāʿī* al-Nakhshabī enjoyed the patronage of the Sāmānid emir Naṣr ibn Aḥmad (914–943) in Bukhara for quite a long time. Al-Muʾayyad, like his father and predecessor before him, was under the protection of the Buwayhid emir Abū Kālījār (1024–1048) in Shīrāz, and Nāṣir-i Khusraw, after his expulsion from Balkh, fled to Yumgān to seek the protection of ʿAlī ibn al-Asad, the emir of Badakhshān. In Multan (in present-day Pakistan), the *daʿwa* also appears to have been established thanks to the fact that the local dynasty of Arab origins, the Banū Munabbih, had been converted to Ismailism and offered their protection to the emissaries of the imam-caliph of Cairo.

These were strokes of luck for the *daʿwa*. As a rule the mission had to operate under difficult conditions, in hostile surroundings, and often under cover. There was no lack of setbacks, as shown by the expulsion of Abū Ḥātim al-Rāzī from Rayy, al-Nakhshabī's catastrophe in Bukhara or Nāṣir-i Khusraw's flight from Balkh. Founding and leading an Ismaili community in a non-Ismaili environment demanded high intellectual and moral capacities, extraordinary skill, as well as subtle political intuition on the part of the leading *dāʿī*. Our text very emphatically shows this:

> For this reason the *dāʿī* must combine in himself all the ideal qualities and talents which may separately be found in the people of different professions and standing. He must possess the good qualities of an expert lawyer (*faqīh*), because he often has to act as a judge; he must possess patience (*ṣabr*), good theoretical education (*ʿilm*), intelligence, psychological insight, honesty, high moral character, sound judgement, etc. He must possess the virtues of leaders, such as a strong will, generosity, administrative talent, tact and tolerance. He must be in possession of the high qualities of the priest, because he has to lead the esoteric prayer of his followers. He must be

> irreproachably honest and reliable, because the most precious thing, the salvation of the souls of many people, is entrusted to him. He should be a real *mujāhid*, a warrior for the religious cause, in his heart, ready to sacrifice his life and everything for the religion. He must have the virtue of the physician, who delicately and patiently treats the sick, because he himself has to heal sick souls. Similarly, he has to possess the virtues of an agriculturist, of a shepherd, of the captain of a ship, of a merchant and the like, developing in himself the good qualities required in different professions.[1]

It goes without saying that the *dāʿī* must have an equally perfect knowledge of the *ẓāhir* and the *bāṭin*. He must, therefore, be a trained jurist (*faqīh*), for in cases of internal conflicts and disputes, the followers (i.e. the Ismailis) are instructed as far as possible to refrain from applying to local judges who do not follow the Ismaili confession (*madhhab*). So within his community the *dāʿī* assumes the office of judge (*qāḍī*), enabling the community to steer clear of the jurisdiction of the ruling regime. This, of course, demands the solidarity of the community. The followers should submit to the judgement of the *dāʿī* and, even if the verdict is to their detriment, they should not try to have it altered by the *qāḍī* of the ruling regime.

Apart from knowledge of strictly religious matters – the Qurʾan, the commentary on the Qurʾan (*tafsīr*), the Traditions of the Prophet (*ḥadīth*), stories of the prophets (*qiṣaṣ al-anbiyāʾ*), and the Ismaili interpretation of these writings (*taʾwīl*) – the ideal *dāʿī* is expected to have an almost encyclopaedic culture: logic and philosophy, history and geography belong equally to his accomplishments so that he may be equipped for any discussion among scholars, prepared for any argument, and unbeatable in any field of erudition. Here again we notice the great respect paid by the Ismailis to all kinds of culture and knowledge:

> The *dāʿī* has to know the ranks and grades of scholars (*ahl al-ʿilm*) and appreciate and honour them. He must not notice whether they are poorly and shabbily clothed, for the souls of scholars are great

> and proud and cannot bear insult and disregard ... Whoever despises them makes himself despicable. When people notice that scholars are highly esteemed, they themselves yearn for knowledge and start studying.[2]

Al-Naysābūrī's treatise, *al-Risāla al-mūjaza*, provides a reasonably good picture of the household of the *dāʿī* at his place of activity. The text presents him as having a rather large household, suggesting that the *dāʿī* belonged to the wealthy and prominent personalities of his city: he had a large family of wives and children, as well as servants and assistants. Of course, he and his dependents had to avoid anything that might lead to evil gossip, such as quarrels or indecent jokes; their reputation had to be and remain spotless. In the choice of his staff members – door-keeper, steward, secretary – he had to make sure of absolute secrecy and reliability. Only initiated Ismaili fellow-believers could be considered for these functions, since there were constant discussions about religious matters in the house. In addition to the family members and the domestic staff, there is also mention of certain people described as *muhājirūn*, those who had made a *hijra* as the Prophet Muḥammad had once done; that is abandoned their home, their family and all their property to emigrate to the seat of the *dāʿī* and put themselves at his service. We may assume that it was from among such highly motivated followers that the group of the closest collaborators and subordinates of the *dāʿī* – in other words, the nucleus of the *daʿwa* – was recruited.

Of course, the same care that was taken in the choice of the domestic staff was also required in the appointment of the subordinate *dāʿī*s, the *maʾdhūn*s and the *mukāsir*s, and above all in selecting the couriers. 'Most disasters are caused by unreliable couriers.' The *dāʿī* had to have constant control over his subordinates. He had to be constantly in a position to travel, so that he could regularly inspect his district. Indispensable for all *dāʿī*s, no matter of what rank, was a knowledge of the local language. When he had to do missionary work in a sectarian or even non-Islamic milieu – for instance, in the Indian subcontinent – the *dāʿī* had to have a thorough knowledge of the foreign confession or religion, in order to adjust his proselytizing efforts to the peculiarities of the milieu.

All these qualifications were required so that the *dāʿī* could be fully integrated into the society in which he lived. He was explicitly encouraged to seek contact with the leading personalities of his city and country, as well as with the political and intellectual elite, especially the latter. In debating with non-Ismaili scholars, the *dāʿī* would improve his knowledge. Even if he was already intelligent this would make him more intelligent, and what is more he would acquire practice in the art of debate and argument (*munāẓara, mujādala*). Thirst for knowledge is a virtue: the ignorant man should not be ashamed to ask questions, and even the knowledgeable, when there is something he has ignored, should admit it. It is better, however, for the *dāʿī* to start out by acquiring vast knowledge as well as thorough training in the art of debate before he ventures to engage in arguments with scholars of different faiths, for should the *dāʿī* be defeated in a public debate, should his logical conclusions be disproved and should he run out of arguments, 'then he will fare like Jonas who was devoured by the fish.' A defeat of this kind diminishes the prestige of the *dāʿī* and reduces the success of the *daʿwa*.

It is the task of the subordinates, especially that of the *mukāsir*, to 'work on' those of a different faith until they run out of arguments, until their former *madhhab* is 'broken', and until a clean sweep has been made in their heads, so that the new message of the *daʿwa* can be imprinted in them. But the *mukāsir* only performs the preparatory work; it is for the *dāʿī* to administer to the pupil – once he is ready to be initiated after a three-day fast – the oath of allegiance (*ʿahd* or *mīthāq*) to the imam ruling in Cairo, and to pledge him to keep the secrets (*kitmān al-sirr*). Its revelation, particularly in a country with a hostile population or government, might lead to the death of people or even to the destruction of the entire 'island' (*jazīra*). What he says in his text about the content of the oath corresponds with the formula handed down by al-Maqrīzī and al-Nuwayrī, so that we have here a further confirmation of the authenticity of this formula.

For the initiate, the *dāʿī* regularly held sessions (*majālis*) in his house, a task demanding pedagogical skills. He had to adjust his lectures to the capacities and intelligence of the particular public with which he was dealing – another peculiarity of the Ismaili *daʿwa* that we have already encountered in several of the sources quoted above. The instruction was administered to the adept in carefully calculated doses, 'just as a child is not given too much food to begin with so that he does not die.' The *dāʿī* should not withhold from the initiate the knowledge he is entitled to, but he should not overfeed him lest this cause confusion in his head which might lead to doubts or even to apostasy. All the questions of the initiate should be answered by the *dāʿī*, though this should be done in accordance with the understanding and the degree of the questioner, neither above nor below his intellectual level. For every believer is entitled to the *entire* truth; the *dāʿī*, being himself the trustee of the entrusted good (*amāna*) mentioned in the Qur'an, has the duty to restore it *completely*, that is fully, to his pupils; he must not withhold even the smallest part of it, for that would mean misappropriating the entrusted knowledge.

For the already initiated faithful 'brothers', the *dāʿī* was to arrange appointed days for consultations apart from the regular *majālis*, but his house had to be open to all believers, men and women alike, at all times. This made the careful choice of the door-man (*bawwāb*) all the more important, for he even had to treat visitors who came at inconvenient times in a polite and friendly manner, and not dismiss them curtly.

In his community the *dāʿī* was also in charge of what is called 'pastoral care' by Christians: he called on the sick, paid visits of condolence in the event of deaths or other misfortunes, personally participated in funerals, and sent congratulatory messages on joyful occasions such as engagements, weddings or the return of a family member from a long journey. A polite, friendly and modest behaviour towards everyone was an important characteristic of the perfect *dāʿī*.

But with all his mildness and friendliness, he had to have a good grip on his 'island'. He had to command respect, otherwise he would not be able to assert himself; and when the need arose, he also had to resort to punishment. The art of controlling people (*siyāsa*) was required of him to a high degree, and the only way to acquire it was by learning how to control himself (*siyāsat nafsih*).

Al-Naysābūrī only very briefly discusses the training of the subordinate *dāʿīs* although his treatise is one of the extremely rare sources containing concrete statements on the subject. The superior *dāʿī* examined the person he had selected as the future *dāʿī* by having him educate initiates in his own presence, so that his examination was a kind of trial *majlis*. If the candidate passed this test, the *dāʿī* raised his rank and assigned him a place in his immediate surroundings, that is, he made him into a kind of assistant who would probably accompany his chief on inspection trips and perhaps also be assigned daily administrative duties such as correspondence and dealing with couriers. Then he would gradually promote him to higher ranks until he was capable of independently assuming the *daʿwa* of a village or of a comparatively large district.

All these tasks demanded from the *dāʿī* a high measure of responsibility and initiative. Living far away in Badakhshān or in Sind, he could not consult the imam in Cairo whenever a problem arose. To accomplish his tasks he needed money; so in the name of the imam he collected the statutory dues from the followers: the alms (*zakāt*) and the one-fifth tax (*khums*) prescribed by the Qurʾan, as well as the duties mentioned above as exclusively applying to the Ismailis (*najwā* and *fiṭra*). Only a part of this money was paid to the treasury (*bayt al-māl*) of the imam-caliph in Cairo. We can imagine how difficult it must have been to send this money from certain remote 'islands' by sea or by land to Egypt. Most of these revenues remained on the spot, at the disposal of the *dāʿī*, who was to use the money for the purposes of the *daʿwa*. Of course, he was not allowed to waste the revenue of the imam, to whom he was accountable. Nor was he allowed to be stingy with the money entrusted to him, for stinginess was detrimental to the purposes of the *daʿwa*, and such vices would reflect badly on the *dāʿī*.

Couriers from Cairo are often mentioned in our treatise, and the *dāʿī* could also send messengers to the court of the imam. The followers, however, were advised to refrain from unnecessarily annoying the imam with their petty problems; besides, they were not to take any independent action, but should avail themselves of the intervention of the *dāʿī* and observe certain time-frames apparently prescribed by Cairo, and even then only in particular emergencies.

If a *dāʿī* was incapable of conducting the *daʿwa* in the manner described, then the faith of the followers would be destroyed. They would turn away from truth and become antinomians or materialists. They would start having doubts about religion, and this would lead to disputes and conflicts. Virtues would be lost, men would become animals and the 'islands' would go to ruin. Then the imam would be disgusted with these members of his community and would turn away from them in his disappointment. It was up to the *dāʿī*s to prevent such dire consequences.

We have no other source from the Fatimid period that provides us with such detailed illustrations of the daily work of the *dāʿī* – albeit couched in an idealized form – as al-

Naysābūrī's *al-Risāla al-mūjaza.* Even if conditions were not always as ideal as they are presented by the author, we may safely assume that the organization of the *daʿwa* functioned efficiently for several centuries in the remotest regions and under the most difficult circumstances. There could be no other explanation for the astonishing achievements of the Ismaili mission.

SIX

Al-Ḥākim's 'House of Knowledge'

The accomplishments of the ideal *dāʿī* as required by al-Naysābūrī in his treatise far exceed the scope of religious knowledge as such. As we have already noted, the ideal *dāʿī* was expected to have an encyclopaedic knowledge of diverse disciplines, for he might at any time be confronted by an opponent versed in one or several of these disciplines who, if he were uneducated, might easily outdo and ridicule him.

The Islamic world of the Middle Ages had no cultural institution that might offer an encyclopaedic knowledge of this kind. Though it is true that with the *madrasa* it had created a cultural institution of high quality and standard, teaching at the *madrasa* was always limited to *religious* knowledge. The instruction and study of medicine or astronomy, algebra or geometry, took place elsewhere in the often private circles of authorities in each of these sciences. The medieval Islamic world was superior to Europe in the same period in all scientific disciplines; but contrary to a position that has often been maintained, it had no institution that united all the disciplines under one roof – in other words, it had no university.

There was one exception. The sixth Fatimid caliph and the sixteenth imam of the Ismailis, al-Ḥākim (996–1021), founded the House of Knowledge (Dār al-ʿIlm) in Cairo in the year 1005. This was also sometimes misleadingly called the House of Wisdom (Dār al-Ḥikma) – misleadingly insofar as 'wisdom' (*ḥikma*) was usually understood as the specific Ismaili esoteric knowledge, the *bāṭin* communicated by the imam through the *dāʿīs*. Al-Ḥākim's institution, however, did not serve the *daʿwa*, but above all those who specialized in the non-religious sciences.

The institute founded by the Fatimid caliph was not the first of its kind. Already in the pre-Islamic period, around the year 555, the great Sasanid king Khusraw Anūshīrwān had established, in the city of Jundaysābūr (in the south-western province of Khūzistān of present-day Iran, near the Iraqi border), a kind of scientific academy which attracted learned men of all disciplines – in particular medicine and philosophy – and of all countries. This institute, which also included a hospital, survived well into the Islamic period, and it was here that the first specifically astronomical observations with precision instruments were carried out at the end of the ninth century.

The Jundaysābūr Academy then served the Abbasid caliph al-Ma'mūn (813–833) as a model for his 'wisdom cabinet' (*bayt al-ḥikma*), which he installed in a wing of his palace in Baghdad, with its library open to scholars of different languages and origins. Al-Ma'mūn's *bayt al-ḥikma* was not so much a university as it was a library and place of work for scholars, whose main task consisted of translating philosophical and scientific works of Greek authors into Arabic. It included an astronomical observatory (*marṣad*) which the caliph had erected near the Shammāsiyya Gate in Baghdad, and the observations made here, based on the earlier works of Greek and Indian astronomers, led to remarkably accurate results, such as the incline of the ecliptic, the precession of the equinoxes and the exact length of the solar year. In addition to the observatory in Baghdad, al-Ma'mūn also had another built on the Qasyūn mountain near Damascus.

These installations seem to have declined soon after the caliph's death. At any rate, they were not the direct prototype for the establishment founded by the Fatimid al-Ḥākim. Its actual model was the Dār al-ʿIlm which the Persian vizier Abū Naṣr Sābūr ibn Ardashīr founded during the Buwayhid reign in the year 991 or 993 in al-Karkh, a southern suburb of Baghdad inhabited by the Shiʿa. This institution included a library with more than 10,000 books.

It may be assumed that al-Ḥākim had detailed information about this institute through his *dāʿīs* who worked in Iraq – at the time al-Kirmānī must have lived in Baghdad – and that he was in this way encouraged to promote the sciences in his own empire in a similar or even more generous manner and to raise the cultural level of his followers. His Dār al-ʿIlm dates only about twelve years later than that of the Baghdad vizier; it was founded on 24 March 1005. Here is an account by al-Ḥākim's intimate friend and court chronicler al-Musabbiḥī (quoted by al-Maqrīzī):

> On this Saturday ... the so-called House of Knowledge in Cairo was inaugurated. The jurists took up residence there, and the books from the palace libraries were moved into it. People could visit it, and whoever wanted to copy something that interested him could do so; the same was true of anyone who wanted to read any of the material kept in it. After the building was furnished and decorated, and after all the doors and passages were provided with curtains, lectures were held there by the Qur'an readers, astronomers, grammarians and philologists, as well as physicians. Guardians, servants, domestics and others were hired to serve there.
>
> Into this house they brought all the books that the commander of the faithful al-Hākim bi-Amr Allāh ordered to bring there, that is, the manuscripts in all the domains of science and culture, to an extent to which they had never been brought together for a prince. He allowed access to all this to people of all walks of life, whether they wanted to read books or dip into them. One of the already mentioned blessings, the likes of which had been unheard of, was also that he granted substantial salaries to all those who were appointed by him there to do service – jurists and others. People from all walks of life visited the House; some came to read books,

others to copy them, and yet others to study. He also donated what people needed: ink, writing reeds, paper and inkstands. The house was [formally] that of the Slav Mukhtār.[1]

The 'Slav' Mukhtār referred to in this passage had belonged to that Fatimid army corps which consisted of slaves of European origin, who were indiscriminately called 'Slavs' (Ṣaqlabī, plural Ṣaqāliba); he had been steward of the caliph's castle under al-Ḥākim's predecessor, the caliph al-ʿAzīz. We know exactly where his house was situated. On its northern side it abutted on the western-most of the two palaces facing one another in the centre of Cairo; this smaller western palace was the residence of the appointed crown-prince. The building no longer exists, but its situation within the townscape of Cairo can still be located since the surviving Aqmar Mosque, which adjoined the large eastern palace, stood exactly opposite it.

The kinds of disciplines taught at the Dār al-ʿIlm can be clearly inferred from the above-quoted text by al-Musabbiḥī, the only contemporary source on the subject. Among the scholars mentioned in connection with this institute are the Qurʾan readers (*qurrāʾ*), jurists (*fuqahāʾ*) and experts on tradition (*muḥaddithūn*), philologists and grammarians, physicians and logicians, mathematicians and astronomers.

The surviving fragments of al-Musabbiḥī's lost chronicle enable us to follow the work of al-Ḥākim's academy over a fairly long period. Under the year 1012–13 al-Musabbiḥī reports: 'From the House of Knowledge a number of mathematicians, logicians and jurists, as well as several physicians were summoned by al-Ḥākim; the representatives of each discipline appeared before him separately, in order to argue in his presence; thereupon he presented all of them with robes of honour and gifts.'[2] The most prominent man of letters whom al-Ḥākim tried to attract to his institute was the blind poet Abū al-ʿAlāʾ al-Maʿarrī (973–1058), who lived in the small town of Maʿarrat al-Nuʿmān in northern Syria. In a letter to the emir of Aleppo, al-Ḥākim invited al-Maʿarrī, one of the major poets of the Arabic language, to Cairo, but he declined.

To begin with, the Dār al-ʿIlm lecturers were remunerated, as we have seen, with salaries (*rizq*) paid from the treasury; this was how the jurists teaching at the Azhar Mosque had already been paid under the caliph al-ʿAzīz and his vizier Ibn Killis. Five years later, however, in April or May 1010, al-Ḥākim placed the institute he had founded on an entirely new economic basis by incorporating it into a larger endowment (*waqf*) which he had provided for the three major mosques of Cairo (al-Azhar, Rāshida and al-Maqs).

The deed of foundation has not come down to us in the original, but the Egyptian chronicler al-Maqrīzī quotes two relatively long fragments from it, giving us detailed information about the endowment of the Dār al-ʿIlm. From his private property (*milk*), the imam-caliph al-Ḥākim donated several estates and concerns in al-Fusṭāṭ (Old Cairo) for the maintenance of the al-Azhar mosque, the mosque in Rāshida and the Dār al-ʿIlm; the mosque in the al-Maqs quarter was to receive separate proceeds. These immovables were the old mint, the market-hall for precious woollen fabrics (*qaysariyyat al-ṣūf*) and another building in the market area (*sūq*) of the old city. The part of the deed concerning al-Azhar contains no further reference to any teaching activity there, so it may be assumed that most if not all the lessons were now concentrated at the new Dār al-ʿIlm.

The proceeds of the above immovables were first of all to be used for the upkeep of the buildings, so as to guarantee the continuance of the endowment. The surplus was then to be divided into sixty equal parts, out of which the Dār al-ʿIlm was to receive 'one-tenth and one eighth of a tenth' – altogether 257 gold dinars a year. The fragment of the deed quoted by al-Maqrīzī precisely pinpoints how this money was to be used:

> for the purchase of mats and other household effects, 10 dinars; for paper for the scribe, i.e. the copyist, 90 dinars – that is the greatest single item – 'for the librarian 48 dinars; for the purchase of water 12, for the servant 15, for paper, ink and writing reeds for the scholars studying there 12; for repairing the curtains 1 dinar; for the repair of possibly torn books or loose leaves 12; for the purchase of felt for blankets in the winter 5; for the purchase of carpets in the winter 4 dinars ...[3]

At this point the fragment of the deed unfortunately breaks off; the sum of the items listed here adds up to 209 dinars only, and we remain uninformed about the distribution of the remaining 48 dinars.

The most important scientific achievement produced by al-Ḥākim's institute was an astronomical chart (*zīj*) with comparative data about stars and planets, *al-zīj al-Ḥākimī*, named after the caliph by its author, the astronomer Aḥmad ibn Yūnus al-Ḥākimī. This *zīj*, called 'al-Ḥākim's Tables', replaced the earlier *zīj* established by the astronomers of the Abbasid caliph al-Ma'mūn with the help of the observatories in Baghdad and Damascus. Al-Ḥākim's astronomers did not have an observatory at their disposal, for the one that al-Ḥākim's supreme *qāḍī*, Mālik ibn Sa'īd, started building in the year 1012 was not completed and remained unused for almost a century as we shall see below. At once a physician, astronomer, mathematician and philosopher, Ibn al-Haytham was the most accomplished of the scientists who served under al-Ḥākim. His pioneering work on optics had far-reaching influences on European thinkers of medieval times, among whom he came to be known as Alhazen. His studies were also of major importance for astrological and meteorological investigations.

After the mysterious disappearance of the caliph al-Ḥākim in the year 1021, we learn nothing more of the scientific results achieved by the Dār al-'Ilm. Under the two succeeding caliphs, al-Ẓāhir (1021–1036) and al-Mustanṣir (1036–1094), the institute no longer seems to have played any significant role. It apparently fell victim to the overall crisis which the Fatimid state underwent in the middle of the eleventh century and which led in the late 1060s to complete anarchy in Egypt.

When in the months of November and December 1068, soldiers and officials who had remained unpaid for some time plundered the palaces and treasuries of the caliph, the libraries were not spared either; for the plunderers, manuscript books were objects of no less value than the jewels of the treasuries. Accounts of this event provide interesting information about the rich contents of both the palace and the academy.

At first the marauders plundered the library in the caliph's palace:

> From it 18,000 volumes on antique sciences were robbed; in addition, 2,400 Qur'an manuscripts with gold and silver illumination; all these were hauled away by the Turkish soldiers … In the month of Muḥarram, twenty-five camels loaded with books made their way on a single day from the palace to the house of the vizier Abū al-Faraj Muḥammad ibn Ja'far, and the latter, as well as [the former vizier] al-Khaṭīr ibn al-Muwaffaq, divided up these books in their two houses [as compensation] for their services, for which the *dīwān* owed them and their employees money. The share of the vizier Abū al-Faraj was valued at 50,000 dinars, but was in reality worth more than 100,000 dinars …

But Abū al-Faraj was not destined to enjoy his booty for long. When, a month later, he himself had to flee Egypt, his house was also plundered, and the books he had appropriated were scattered to the four winds.[4]

The Dār al-'Ilm hardly fared any better:

> The library of the Dār al-'Ilm in Cairo was also emptied. Many books came into the possession of a certain 'Imād al-Dawla Abū al-Faḍl ibn al-Muḥtariq in Alexandria; but when the latter was murdered, many of them were taken to the Maghrib. The Berbers of the Luwāta tribe [who lived as nomads on the western edge of the Nile Delta and in present-day Libya] acquired countless indescribably beautiful books through purchase or robbery and took them with them. Their slaves and maids used the covers to make

> sandals for their feet; as for the leaves, they burnt them because they came from the palace; for they believed that they contained the religious doctrines of the Orientals [i.e. the Ismailis], which contradicted their own [Sunni] religious doctrines. The ashes formed great hills in the province of Ibyār [in the Nile Delta], which are even today called the 'Hills of Books' (*tilāl al-kutub*). Many books were thrown into the river or were otherwise destroyed, but many of them reached the great metropolises [of other countries].[5]

The original Dār al-ʿIlm of the caliph al-Ḥākim was thus destroyed. The empty building was used for other purposes. We read that in the year 1074 – that is, ten years after the great plunder – the chief *dāʿī* al-Muʾayyad al-Shīrāzī was buried in the Dār al-ʿIlm. This leads us to conclude that he had lived and worked there for some time. Perhaps the building had been assigned to him as an office.

SEVEN

Scientific Institutions under the Fatimids

By relating the story of the plundering of the 'House of Knowledge', we have already to a certain extent anticipated later events in the history of the Fatimid dynasty. When the imam-caliph al-Ḥākim disappeared in February 1021 his energetic elder sister, Sitt al-Mulk, became the regent, since al-Ḥākim's only son 'Alī – the caliph al-Ẓāhir (1021–1036) – was only fifteen years old at the time. The organization of the Ismaili *daʿwa*, which during the Druze disorders threatened to disintegrate from within, was re-established. Qāsim, a great-grandson of al-Qāḍī al-Nuʿmān, was appointed chief *dāʿī* (*dāʿī al-duʿāt*) and by an edict of al-Ẓāhir the sessions of wisdom (*majālis al-ḥikma*) were re-opened. Princess Sitt al-Mulk, who counts among the foremost female figures of Islamic history, reigned for only two years. She died at the age of fifty-two on 5 February 1023 (Dhu'l-Qaʿda 413)[1] and a camarilla of courtiers under the leadership of the black eunuch, Miʿḍād, governed, or rather misgoverned, on behalf of the under-age caliph. This period also marked the beginning of the career of the Iraqi-born state secretary, 'Alī b. Aḥmad al-Jarjarā'ī, who had had both his hands cut off on al-Ḥākim's order because he had illicitly opened a report from the secret service and tampered with it. Despite this handicap he rose to the highest offices under al-Ẓāhir and became vizier in the year 1027. He held this office for seventeen years, even after the reign of al-Ẓāhir and until his own death in 1045.

During the reign of al-Ẓāhir the Fatimid empire was shaken by severe internal crises. Inadequate Nile levels caused several years of famine. In Palestine and Syria there were Bedouin rebellions which were put down by the capable general, Anūshtikīn al-Dizbirī, after hard battles. It was thanks to him that the Fatimid reign over Syria was re-established. After his victory over the Bedouins, near Uqḥuwāna in Palestine in the year 1029, he also managed to reconquer Aleppo in 1038 and to stabilize the Fatimid empire up to the Euphrates.

In June 1036 the caliph al-Ẓāhir died of the plague at the age of thirty-one, and his son, Maʿadd al-Mustanṣir bi'llāh, succeeded to the throne at the age of seven. Once more it was the viziers who led the government on behalf of the under-age caliph; first al-Jarjarāʾī until his death in 1045, then from 1050 to 1058 al-Ḥasan b. ʿAlī al-Yāzūrī, who combined in his hands the offices of supreme *qāḍī*, supreme *dāʿī* and vizier. During this period the Ismaili *daʿwa* achieved a spectacular, though only temporary, success in Iraq. Here the Ismaili *dāʿī* al-Muʾayyad al-Shīrāzī managed to take advantage of the disorders following the fall of the Buwayhids (1055) to step up the propaganda for the Fatimid caliph, so that by the beginning of the year 1057, al-Mustanṣir was acknowledged as caliph in Mawṣil (Mosul) on the Tigris, in Wāsiṭ and in Kūfa on the Euphrates. At the end of 1058 this also applied to Baghdad, where pro-Fatimid troops soon marched in under General al-Basāsīrī. The Abbasid caliph, al-Qāʾim, was forced to abdicate and was deported to ʿĀna on the Euphrates. His cloak and other insignia of sovereignty were sent to Cairo. This was the greatest victory of the Fatimids. At last they had realized the aim towards which they had so long aspired. The Abbasid dynasty of the 'usurpers' had fallen, and Baghdad had become part of the Fatimid empire. The leader of the Ismaili *daʿwa* in Iraq, al-Muʾayyad al-Shīrāzī, rose to the office of chief *dāʿī*, thus crowning his career with a twofold victory. But this triumph was soon gambled away by Ibn al-Maghribī, the incompetent successor to the vizier al-Yāzūrī, who denied al-Basāsīrī urgently needed financial and military assistance. And so in December 1059, when the Abbasid caliphate was restored with the help of the Turkish Saljuqs, the latter had to leave Baghdad again.

The pendulum quickly swung to the other side. From the year 1062 Egypt sank into total anarchy. Within the Fatimid armies, the Turkish and Berber troops constantly fought with the contingents of the black slave troops. A Turkish officer seized power and, in the year 1070 in Alexandria, even acknowledged the Abbasid caliph of Baghdad as sovereign of Egypt. Unfortunately, the level of the Nile flood remained below average during the years 1065 to 1072 and the 'seven meagre years' of the biblical Joseph seemed to have returned. Famine, dearth and epidemics were the usual consequences. Unpaid soldiers roamed through the country, plundering and devastating it. They finally forced the caliph al-Mustanṣir to open the treasury and even the libraries, which were completely ransacked. We have seen how al-Ḥākim's famous 'House of Knowledge' was also ruined in these troubled times. The palaces of the Fatimids were similarly robbed and emptied. It is reported that the women of the harem went begging in the streets and that the caliph al-Mustanṣir himself sat on a shabby mat in an empty room of his ransacked palace, kept alive solely by the care of a pious woman of Sharīfian descent who spent the remains of her fortune to provide the imam-caliph with minimum provisions.

The terrible years that Egypt experienced in the sixth decade of the eleventh century came to an end when, in the year 1074, Badr al-Jamālī, an Armenian officer, re-stabilized the

Fatimid empire and ushered in the last great period of the Fatimid caliphate. Badr al-Jamālī (governed 1074–1094) was at the same time vizier and commander-in-chief of the armies (*amīr al-juyūsh*); in other words, he combined in his hands both the supreme civil and military powers. In his time the old mud-brick wall of Cairo, which had been built by Jawhar when the city was founded, was replaced by the stone walls and gates that even today lend the old city of Cairo its characteristic aspect: the 'Gate of Triumphs' (Bāb al-Futūḥ), the 'Victory Gate' (Bāb al-Naṣr) to the north and the Zawīla or Zuwayla Gate (Bāb Zuwayla) to the south.

The caliph al-Mustanṣir, the 18th imam of the Ismailis, died soon after Badr in December 1094 after a rule of almost sixty years (1036–1094). His son and appointed successor, Nizār, was driven from the throne, imprisoned and murdered. A collateral line of the Fatimid dynasty ascended the throne of Cairo and ruled Egypt, Palestine and Syria until the dynasty ended in the year 1171. This line, beginning with the caliph al-Mustaʿlī (1094–1101) has not been recognized as Imams by the 'Nizārī' Ismailis of Iran, Syria, Central Asia, India and other regions. The person responsible for these events and for the schism connected with them, the splitting up of the Ismaili movement into Nizārīs and Mustaʿlīs, was Badr al-Jamālī's son, al-Afḍal (governed 1094–1121). He enjoyed the same full powers as his father which he used to enforce the succession of Nizār's youngest brother, al-Mustaʿlī, who was also married to his sister.

Under the caliph al-Mustaʿlī's son and successor, al-Āmir (1101–1130), the former House of Knowledge (Dār al-ʿIlm) once again caused a stir. In the year 1119 a group of sectarians settled in it, about whom the contemporary chronicler Ibn al-Ma'mūn al-Baṭā'iḥī gives us a detailed account. At the head of this group was a certain Ḥamīd ibn al-Makkī from the city of Aṭfīḥ in central Egypt, a dwarf and by profession a fuller (*qaṣṣāb*) who had rallied around himself a following from lower ranks, mainly employees from the palace and artisans from the *sūq*. Regarding the religious doctrines of these people, who called themselves the Unparalleled (al-Badīʿiyya), our source unfortunately contains nothing but vague statements. Like the famous mystic Manṣūr al-Ḥallāj (d. 922), Ḥamīd was said to have called himself divine. The dictator al-Afḍal thereupon had the dubious circle evicted and the building closed down. However, another source, Ibn ʿAbd al-Ẓāhir, gives a different reason for closing down the building, namely that al-Afḍal feared 'that there might be meetings held there in the spirit of the Nizārī doctrine.'[2]

In the year 1121 the caliph al-Āmir had his minister, al-Afḍal, killed by assassins and took over the affairs of state himself. Soon afterwards the dwarf Ḥamīd and his companions were again up to their usual mischief in the building of the former Dār al-ʿIlm. One of the leading Ismaili *dāʿīs*, Ibn ʿAbd al-Ḥaqīq, complained about the situation to the new vizier, al-Maʾmūn al-Baṭāʾiḥī (the father of our informant), who in February 1123 had the entire company of the 'Unparalleled' arrested and called upon to revoke their false doctrines; whoever refused was executed.

So the building stood empty again. 'Thereupon the caliph al-Āmir ordered the vizier al-Maʾmūn al-Baṭāʾiḥī to take possession of the Dār al-ʿIlm and to re-open it in accordance with its lawful destinations.' What he meant by 'lawful destinations' (*al-awḍāʿ al-sharʿiyya*) was apparently al-Ḥākim's pious endowment (*waqf*), which was indeed enacted for all eternity until the Last Judgement, and which was now re-established. This serves as an impressive example for the deep-rootedness of the Fatimid traditions of learning.

According to the account of the chronicler Ibn ʿAbd al-Ẓāhir, the caliph al-Āmir consulted his advisers about the best site for the new Dār al-ʿIlm. When somebody suggested that the old building be used again, the vizier al-Baṭāʾiḥī argued that the old house north of the Little Palace was quite unsuitable, for it had for a long time been used as a gateway to the palace, and the constant comings and goings would be detrimental to teaching activities. Since the caliph did not want to have the institute within his own palace, the steward finally suggested a spacious building complex in the vicinity of the great eastern palace (in the area today called Khān al-Khalīlī); it was here that the 'New House of Knowledge' (Dār al-ʿIlm al-Jadīda) was accommodated. The vizier stipulated 'that its director must be a pious man and that the supreme *dāʿī* should supervise it.' He apparently feared a revival of dissident activities. A certain Abū Muḥammad Ḥasan ibn Ādam was appointed as the director, and several Qur'an reciters (*muqriʾūn*) were assigned to him. In May 1132 the House was inaugurated, and it continued to operate until the end of the Fatimid dynasty in the year 1171, that is for a period of forty-eight years.

Apart from this brief account by the chronicler Ibn ʿAbd al-Ẓāhir, quoted by al-Maqrīzī,[3] we have no further information about the new Dār al-ʿIlm. As far as its scientific significance is concerned, it seems not to have borne comparison with the Imam al-Ḥākim's first Dār al-ʿIlm. It may indeed have been no more than a *dār al-qirāʾa*, for apart from the Qur'an reciters no scholars of other disciplines are mentioned, and we know of no renowned scientist working there. No doubt the Dār al-ʿIlm must have been used for the Ismaili (Mustaʿlian) *daʿwa* – as it had been at the time of the supreme *dāʿī* al-Muʾayyad al-Shīrāzī – for the late Fatimid historian, Ibn al-Ṭuwayr, incidentally mentions that the Ismaili scholars (*fuqahāʾ*) attached to the supreme *dāʿī* had a house called Dār al-ʿIlm. The deposition of the last Fatimid caliph, al-ʿĀḍid, in the year 1171 brought about the definitive end of this institute that had been so grandiosely planned by its founder, al-Ḥākim.

As al-Ḥākim's academy disappeared, another of his plans was realized in later Fatimid times; this was the construction of an observatory on the Muqaṭṭam hills, east of Cairo. The belief that the movements of planets against the background of the star-filled sky are of fateful significance to the life of man is as old as the wish to read one's future destiny from particular constellations. In its main features, astrology goes back to the Babylonians, who thought that the seven planets – among which they also counted the sun and the moon, but not the earth – were gods whose intentions mankind could explore by carefully observing their movements. The Greeks and Romans adopted this belief and handed it down both to the Islamic and the Western worlds. In all European languages, the names of the seven days of the week still preserve those of pagan Roman or Germanic gods (in English, for instance, Thursday, the day of Thor, the god of thunder; Friday, the day of the goddess Freya; in French: Vendredi, the day of the goddess Venus, etc.).

Such conceptions are absolutely incompatible with the monotheism of Judaism, Christianity and Islam. The belief in a single God as the creator and ruler of the world excludes the idea of blindly ruling powers of fate. Yet astrology has tenaciously survived as a sediment of superstition in both Christian and Islamic civilizations.

But already with the Babylonians – and later with the Greeks – the hope of discovering the future was combined with a scientific interest in the universe and in the exact movements of the celestial bodies, in other words, in astronomy. Both existed side by side in a hardly separable mixture; the medieval astronomers, whether eastern or western, were for the most part astrologers as well. Even the great German astronomer Johannes Kepler (1571–1630) earned his income with horoscopes for princes and kings; and in Arabic the word *al-munajjim* means both astronomer and astrologer.

However, the awareness always existed that traditional pagan residues were incompatible with the monotheistic faith. This applies to the Christian church, which often turned against astrological superstition, as well as to the Muslim *ʿulamāʾ*. It also applies to the Ismailis, whose imams and *dāʿīs* repeatedly pronounced explicit verdicts against astrology.

The best example was set by the first Fatimid caliph al-Mahdī. When on 12 October 909, after his solemn enthronement in Sijilmāsa (in present-day Morocco), he started off eastwards on his way to Qayrawān, the astrologers warned him of an adverse constellation – Mars in the ascendant, the constellation of Virgo – but the imam did not believe in astrology. He ignored the warning and answered the astrologers: 'We march in the name of God and His victory! Mars and the empire are ours!'[4]

Equally characteristic of the Fatimids' disdain of astrology are the words of the third Fatimid caliph al-Manṣūr (946–953), as handed down by al-Qāḍī al-Nuʿmān in his book 'Audiences and Rides' (*al-Majālis wa'l-musāyarāt*, § 72):

> Al-Manṣūr came to speak of astronomy, in which he was well versed. And he said to me: 'By God, I have studied it, but not because like other people I wanted to foresee future destinies. Sometimes I foreknew the situations in the battles during the civil war [of Abū Yazīd], which I experienced myself until its end, but it was not that I knew these situations because I thought particularly highly of astrology. On the contrary, it often happened that the actual future event was revealed to my heart, while the predictions of the stars contradicted it and were incompatible with it. So I paid no attention to the predictions and did not worry about them, but acted in accordance with that which was revealed to my heart, and in it there always lay success and victory! By God, we have only studied this science because it leads us to the confession of the oneness of God (*tawḥīd*) and the effects of His wisdom on the deeds of His creation. So beware of occupying yourself with anything else and worrying about anything else![5]

As the Imam al-Manṣūr makes clear, the study of the stars explains God's creation to us; all else is superstition. In several passages the book from which we have just quoted, al-Qāḍī al-Nuʿmān hands down similar verdicts by the imams against astrology (§ 169; 229; 231; 262; 275); and the caliph al-Ḥākim's edict of 1013 against astrology and the astrologers is in the same tradition:

> He forbade idle talk about the stars. Several astrologers thereupon emigrated, but some of them stayed behind. These were banished, and the population was warned against hiding any of them. Then some of the astrologers showed remorse and were forgiven, and they swore that they would never again look at the stars.[6]

Like his great-grandfather al-Manṣūr, however, al-Ḥākim combined scorn for astrology with a particular esteem for scientific astronomy. As we have seen, the latest astronomical tables established in Cairo, *al-zīj al-Ḥākimī*, bore the name of the caliph who had commissioned them. It was in the same spirit that al-Ḥākim ordered an observatory to be built on the Muqaṭṭam mountains east of Cairo.

As already indicated, the Abbasid caliph al-Maʾmūn (813–833) had had two observatories built, one in Baghdad and the other on the al-Qasyūn mountain near Damascus. In the year 988 in Baghdad, the Buwayhid Sharaf al-Dawla Shīrāzī ordered that 'the seven planets be observed in their course through the zodiac, following al-Maʾmūn's example.' This task was undertaken by Ibn Rustam al-Kūhī, a learned astronomer and engineer who built a house in the palace at the rear end of the garden for that purpose.[7] Twenty-four years later, in November or December 1012, al-Ḥākim's supreme *qāḍī* Mālik ibn Saʿīd gave orders for building an observatory (*raṣad*) in the mountains east of Cairo,[8] an initiative he could hardly have taken without the consent of the imam-caliph. The project was not completed, however, and the sources mention no reasons for the failure.

It was the dictator al-Afḍal ibn Badr al-Jamālī (1094–1121) who resumed the work. The incentive for it was the plan to revise the calendar for the beginning of the year 500 of the Hijra, 2 September 1106. This was a task that also had great practical significance, for since the time of the Pharaohs important matters such as sowing and harvesting in Egypt depended on the accuracy of the calendar. While in Egypt the more recent Ḥākim tables were used, in Damascus and the Syrian provinces of the Fatimid empire the obsolete Maʾmūn tables were still employed. The result was that, at the beginning of each year, the astronomers submitted two different calendars, which considerably complicated the work of the administration. To remedy this inconvenience al-Afḍal ordered that al-Ḥākim's plans for the building of an observatory be resumed. The site chosen was a plateau on a spur of the Muqaṭṭam mountains south-east of Cairo, above the cemeteries of al-Qarafa.

About the construction of the observatory we have a detailed account by the contemporary Ibn al-Maʾmūn al-Baṭāʾiḥī, whose father, al-Maʾmūn, at the time an officer and later a vizier, had a prominent part in the project. In a book entitled 'The Building of the Observatory' (*Kitāb ʿamal al-raṣad*) which has not survived but from which extracts are quoted by al-Maqrīzī,[9] Ibn al-Maʾmūn tells the story of the observatory and the series of setbacks that led to the ultimate failure of the project.

The technical task was assigned to the superintendent of arsenals and armouries, Ibn Qirqa (son of George), a Christian physician and scientist. On the plateau he first had the most important part cast in bronze: a circular hoop with a diameter of about 10 yards and a circumference of 30. The first cast miscarried, much to the vexation of the attending al-Afḍal who furiously threw his purse at the workers and was only barely induced to consent to a second attempt since the bronze cast was very expensive.

The second cast was successful, and now the gigantic piece was hoisted onto the flat roof of the nearby Mosque of the Elephant (*masjid al-fīla*). In the middle of the bronze hoop the workers then built a masonry plinth supporting a mast made of oak-wood on which a wooden beam could turn horizontally above the hoop. But when the observatory was completed it was discovered that the sunrise could not be observed from this site, since the much higher eastern crest of the Muqaṭṭam mountains obstructed the view. The efforts of Ibn Qirqa and his men had been in vain.

Thereupon a great deal of labour was mobilized in order to transport the bronze hoop and the mast with the beam to the crest of the mountain and assemble them on the Juyūshī Mosque, which still exists. But first the hand would not turn – it had probably been damaged during the transportation – and had to be replaced. Then the division into degrees and minutes on the bronze hoop warped – the hoop was apparently too heavy and was bent by its own weight. The engineer was reproached for making the hoop too large, but he quite rightly insisted on the principle that the larger the hoop, the more accurate the measurements, adding that if it were technically possible to cast a hoop with one side resting on the Muqaṭṭam and the other on the pyramids, he would build it.

The vizier al-Afḍal took great interest in the work. He had himself transported up the mountain again and again, although he was already shaky with old age and had to recover from the exertion each time he arrived at the top. The difficulties were insurmountable, so the engineer finally gave in and ordered a smaller hoop about 7 yards in diameter and with a circumference of 21 yards to be cast. But before the work could be completed, on the feast of breaking the fast in the year 515 of the Hijra (13 December 1121), al-Afḍal was assassinated and the project was practically abandoned for a while.

The successor to the murdered vizier was al-Ma'mūn al-Baṭā'iḥī, the father of our chronicler. Al-Ma'mūn tried to finish the work, it being his ambition to bequeath to posterity a 'Ma'mūn Observatory' (*al-raṣad al-Ma'mūnī*). But he too failed and his son wrote: 'Had it been God's will that al-Ma'mūn should remain for a little while, the observatory would have been completed, but He took it with Him in the night before Saturday 3 Ramaḍān of the year 519 [3 October 1125].'[10]

Thus ended the last ambitious scientific enterprise of the Fatimid dynasty. The subsequent rulers of Egypt – Ayyubids, Mamluks and Ottomans – showed little ambition in this field, and scientific research took place elsewhere. But although the Ḥākim observatory never started functioning, the caliph's efforts to promote astronomy bore important fruits. The 'Ḥākim Tables', which were commissioned by him and named after him, prevailed and remained in use for several centuries, even outside Egypt and Syria. They had been established without the aid of an observatory, and with smaller though highly precise instruments; but they were sufficiently accurate to compete with the findings of later observatories.

The plunderings of the Fatimid libraries during the year 1068 were compensated for in later years; an Ismaili *daʿwa* without libraries was unimaginable. The fondness of the Ismaili imams for books from a very early stage is again and again emphasized by contemporary sources. Thus al-Mahdī took books with him on his flight from Syria to the Maghrib in the year 905. When his caravan was attacked by Bedouin robbers in the region of today's Libya he lost his books, but several years later they came into his possession again. The third Fatimid caliph, al-Manṣūr (946–953), is described on a hot summer's day sitting in the shade of a tree in one of his country estates, bathed in perspiration, his closely shaven skull uncovered, writing a book. He rejected the advice of his son to resort to a cooler place because that would make him 'lose the thread of his ideas'.[11] His successor, al-Muʿizz (953–975), was infatuated with books. The Qāḍī al-Nuʿmān relates in his 'Audiences and Rides' that al-Muʿizz himself had described how one day he had asked for a certain book he wanted to refer to, but the librarian could not find it. The caliph continued:

> So I went to the library myself, opened one of the cabinets and remained standing at the place where I thought I might find the book; this was at the beginning of night. I examined the books and started leafing through whichever fell into my hands; thus I came upon passages that I wanted to study carefully. Then I reached for another book, and the same thing happened. And so I stood there and looked through one book after another. I no longer knew why I was there and even forgot to sit down. Not until I felt a violent pain in my legs as a result of standing for such a long time did I remember where I was.[12]

After the Fatimids moved to Egypt in the year 973 the palace in Cairo acquired a library unmatched anywhere in the contemporary world. During the reign of al-ʿAzīz (975–996) it contained more than thirty copies of the *al-ʿAyn* dictionary by the well-known grammarian Khalīl (d. 791). The famous world chronicle of al-Ṭabarī (839–923) was represented by twenty copies, as well as an autograph copy; of the major work of the philologist and lexicographer Ibn Durayd (837–933), *al-Jamhara*, there were a hundred copies. When this palace library was plundered by Turkish soldiers in the year 1068 it consisted of forty rooms. The works of classical authors alone comprised 18,000 volumes.

After the total loss of the palace library in the troubles of the year 1068 during the caliphate of al-Mustanṣir, the collections had to be re-assembled and soon they once more comprised a considerable number of volumes. Ibn al-Ṭuwayr, a chronicler of the late Fatimid and early Ayyūbid periods, is our major source on the subject.[13] He writes that the library was situated in one of the rooms of the Little (western) Palace, in which Sultan Saladin installed a hospital (*māristān*) after the fall of the Fatimids (1171). When the Fatimid caliph visited the library he rode his horse from the Great (eastern) Palace and dismounted on a platform (*dikka*) specially built for him. He remained seated on the platform until the librarian brought him the volumes he wanted.

> This library contained a great many bookshelves standing all around the enormous hall; the shelves were divided into compartments by vertical partitions; each compartment was secured by a hinged door with a padlock. There were more than 200,000 bound books and a few without bindings: jurisprudence according to different schools, grammar and philology, books about the traditions of prophets, history, biographies of rulers, astronomy, spiritual knowledge (*rūḥāniyyāt*) and alchemy – on each discipline the [relevant] manuscripts, among them also unfinished ones that were not completed. All this was written on a label attached to the door of each compartment. The venerable Qur'an manuscripts were preserved in a higher place ... Whenever the caliph wanted to pause, he walked around for a while and looked at the shelves. There were two copyists; apart from them two servants: the man with the ladder and another.

After Sultan Ṣalāḥ al-Dīn (Saladin) had deposed the last Fatimid caliph al-ʿĀḍid in the year 1171 the library was sold and the rooms converted into a hospital. The chronicler Ibn Abī Ṭayyiʾ of Aleppo, a Twelver Shiʿi, has left the following account:

> Among the things that were sold was the library. It was one of the wonders of the world, and it was said that in all the lands of Islam there had been no greater library than the one in the palace of Cairo. Among the astonishing things is the fact that there were 1,200 copies of al-Ṭabarī's chronicle and many others! It is said that there were 1,600,000 volumes in it.

The latter figures are most certainly exaggerated; Ibn al-Ṭuwayr mentions the number of books as 200,000, and the Ayyubid chronicler Ibn Wāṣil merely speaks of 'more than 120,000', which seems closer to the truth.

Sultan Saladin had part of the collection sold and part of it destroyed, probably including anything connected with the religious doctrines of the Ismailis. The broker Ibn Sūra – the contemporary Sothebys – brought the smaller part of the library on the market and sold it to individuals. As for the remaining 100,000 volumes, they were entrusted by Saladin to his adviser and intimate friend, al-Qāḍī al-Fāḍil, who left them to the Madrasa al-Fāḍiliyya, which he had founded.

∞ Epilogue ∞

While the literary legacy of the Fatimids in Egypt was dissipated and to a great extent lost, it was preserved by Ismaili communities in their private libraries in all parts of the Islamic world; in the Yemen as well as in India and Pakistan, in Syria as well as in Iran, Afghanistan and Central Asia.

After the schism of the Ismaili community in the year 1094, the Nizārī *daʿwa* had its centre at the Alamūt fortress situated in the mountains of Daylam (between Tehran and the southern coast of the Caspian Sea), which the Fatimid *dāʿī* Ḥasan-i Ṣabbāḥ had taken in the year 1090. We know that Alamūt also had an important library. Ḥasan-i Ṣabbāḥ himself was a distinguished author, but of his writings only a small fragment survives. Under his successors this library must have acquired a significant size.

When in 1256 the last lord of Alamūt, Rukn al-Dīn Khurshāh, surrendered to the Mongol Khan, Hūlāgū, the grandson of Genghis Khan, and the Alamūt fortress capitulated, the library also came to an end. Juwaynī, the vizier of the Khan, reports in his chronicle, 'The History of the World Conqueror':

> Being desirous of inspecting the library, the fame of which had spread throughout the world, I suggested to the King that the valuable books in Alamūt ought not to be destroyed. He approved my words and gave the necessary orders; and I went to examine

> the library, from which I extracted whatever I found in the way of copies of the Koran and [other] choice books after the manner of '*He brought forth the living from the dead*' [Qur'an XXX: 18]. I likewise picked out the astronomical instruments such as, armillary spheres, complete and partial astrolabes and other … that were there. As for the remaining books, which related to their heresy and error and were neither founded on tradition nor supported by reason, I burnt them all.[1]

But the work of destruction was not as complete as the fanatic Juwaynī had meant it to be. The religious literature was handed down to us by the Ismaili communities, and the scientific legacy was also preserved. Naṣīr al-Dīn al-Ṭūsī (d. 1247), who had until then served the Ismailis of Alamūt, became one of the most famous mathematicians and astronomers of his period. By order of his Mongol king he created one of the most modern observatories of his time in Marāgha in the north-western Iranian province of Azerbaijan. It was the first to be equipped with a huge quadrant built of stone. Astronomers from China, Iran, Iraq and Syria worked at this institute and produced new astronomical tables, the 'Ilkhānid Tables' (*al-zīj al-īl-khānī*), thus named after the title of *īl-khān* (prince of the land) which the Mongol rulers of Iran had assumed. Later on, these tables were brought to Muslim Andalusia and, through the Jewish professor Rabbi Abraham ben Samuel Zacuto, to Salamanca and Zaragoza. When the Jews were expelled from Spain, Abraham Zacuto fled to Lisbon to the court of King John II of Portugal. Based on the year 1473, Zacuto created his new tables, the *Almanach perpetuum*, which guided the Portuguese navigators on their expeditions along the west coast of Africa. It was also Zacuto who made the astrolabe which Vasco da Gama carried with him on board his flagship on his first voyage around the Cape of Good Hope to India in 1497–98. So it was the astronomical knowledge of a one-time resident of Alamūt which helped the Europeans find the sea-route to India and usher in the dawn of a new era in world history.

∞ Notes ∞

Chapter 1

1 H. Halm, 'Les Fatimides à Salamya', *Revue des Études Islamiques*, 54 (1986), pp. 133–49.

2 Aḥmad b. Ibrāhīm al-Naysābūrī, *Istitār al-imām*, ed. W. Ivanow, in *Bulletin of the Faculty of Arts, University of Egypt*, 4, part 2 (1936), p. 95; English trans. W. Ivanow, in his *Ismaili Tradition Concerning the Rise of the Fatimids* (London, etc., 1942), p. 162.

3 According to the anonymous *Sīrat al-Imām al-Mahdī*, quoted by Idrīs 'Imād al-Dīn,*'Uyūn al-akhbār*, vol.5, ed. M. Ghālib (Beirut, 1975), p. 89.

4 See W. Ivanow, *The Alleged Founder of Ismailism* (Bombay, 1946).

5 Muḥammad b. Muḥammad al-Yamānī, *Sīrat al-Ḥājib Ja'far b.'Alī*, ed. W. Ivanow, in *Bulletin of the Faculty of Arts, University of Egypt*, 4, part 2 (1936), pp. 107–33; English trans. Ivanow, in his *Ismaili Tradition*, pp. 184–223.

Chapter 2

1 Aḥmad b. 'Abd al-Wahhāb al-Nuwayrī, *Nihāyat al-arab*, vol. 25, ed. M. J. 'A. al-Ḥīnī and 'A. al-Ahwānī (Cairo, 1984), pp. 217–20; Taqī al-Dīn Aḥmad b. 'Alī al-Maqrīzī, *al-Khiṭaṭ* (Bulaq, 1270/1853–54), vol. 1, pp. 396–7; English translation in H. Halm, 'The Isma'ili Oath of Allegiance (*'ahd*) and the Sessions of Wisdom (*majālis al-ḥikma*) in Fatimid Times', in F. Daftary (ed.), *Mediaeval Isma'ili History and Thought* (Cambridge, 1996), pp. 91–115. The texts translated by Bernard Lewis, 'Ismā'īlī Notes', *Bulletin of the School of Oriental and African Studies*, 12 (1947–48), pp. 597 ff., are merely late additions to the original wording of the oath.

2 al-Qāḍī ʿAbd al-Jabbār, *Tathbīt dalāʾil al-nubuwwa*, ed. ʿA.ʿUthmān (Beirut, 1966), p. 595.

3 a*l-Risāla al-mūjaza al-kāfiya fī shurūṭ al-daʿwa al-hādiya* , manuscript published in facsimile, in Verena Klemm, *Die Mission des fāṭimidischen Agenten al-Muʾayyad fī d-dīn in Šīrāz* (Frankfurt, 1989), appendix, pp. 16 and 47.

4 *Kitāb al-ʿālim waʾl-ghulām*, ed. M. Ghālib, in his *Arbaʿ kutub ḥaqqāniyya* (Beirut 1987), pp. 15–75; English paraphrase by W. Ivanow, in his *Studies in Early Persian Ismailism* (2nd ed., Bombay, 1955), pp. 61–86; French translation by H. Corbin, as 'L'initiation ismaélienne ou l'ésotérisme et le Verbe', *Eranos Jahrbuch, 39* (1970), pp. 41–142, reprinted in H. Corbin, *L'Homme et son ange* (Paris, 1983), pp. 81–205.

5 al-Qāḍī al-Nuʿmān, *Iftitāḥ al-daʿwa*, ed. W. al-Qāḍī (Beirut, 1970), pp. 73, 76, 130, 140, ed. F. al-Dashrāwī (Tunis, 1975), pp. 49, 53, 128, 146.

6 Ibn ʿIdhārī, *al-Bayān al-mughrib*, ed. G. S. Colin and E. Lévi-Provençal (New ed., Leiden, 1948–51), p. 132.

7 The author of the *Sīrat al-Mahdī* was probably the *dāʿī* Abū ʿAbd Allāh ibn al-Aswad ibn al-Haytham. The fragments of his work are handed down in Idrīs ʿImād al-Dīn's *ʿUyūn al-akhbār*, vol. 5. See H. Halm, 'Zwei fāṭimidische Quellen aus der Zeit des Kalifen al-Mahdī (909-934)', *Die Welt des Orients*, 19 (1988), pp. 102–17.

8 Idrīs,*ʿUyūn al-akhbār*, vol. 5, p. 137 (= S.M. Stern, *Studies in Early Ismāʿīlism*, Jerusalem-Leiden, 1983, pp. 102 ff.).

9 al-Qāḍī al-Nuʿmān, *Daʿāʾim al-Islām*, ed. A. A. A. Fyzee (Cairo, 1951-61), 2 vols; partial English translation by Fyzee, *The Book of Faith: From the Daʿāʾim al-Islam* (Bombay, 1974).

10 al-Qāḍī al-Nuʿmān, *al-Majālis waʾl-musāyarāt*, ed. Ḥ. al-Faqī et al. (Tunis, 1978), pp. 348, 434, 487, 546.

11 Ibid., p. 487.

12 Ibid., pp. 386–8.

13 al-Qāḍī al-Nuʿmān, *Taʾwīl al-daʿāʾim*, ed. M. Ḥ. al-Aʿẓamī (Cairo, 1967–1972), 3 vols, part I, ed. ʿĀdil al-ʿAwwā, in his *Muntakhabāt Ismāʿīliyya* (Damascus, 1958).

Chapter 3

1 al-Maqrīzī, *Ittiʿāẓ al-ḥunafāʾ*, ed. J. al-Shayyāl and M. Ḥ. M. Aḥmad (Cairo, 1967-1973), vol. 2, pp. 292 ff.

2 Ibid., vol. 2, p. 78.

3 al-Maqrīzī, *Kitāb al-muqaffā al-kabīr*, ed. M. al-Yaʿlāwī (Beirut, 1991), vol. 3, pp. 661 ff.

4 Ḥamīd al-Dīn al-Kirmānī, *Majmūʿat rasāʾil*, ed. M. Ghālib (Beirut, 1983), pp. 134–47.

Chapter 4

1 Quoted by Ibn Khallikān, *Wafayāt al-aʿyān*, ed. I.ʿAbbās (Beirut, 1968–72), vol. 5, p. 416, l. 17.

2 Ibn Ḥajar al-ʿAsqalānī, *Rafʿ al-iṣr*, published in al-Kindī, *Kitāb al-wulāt wa-kitāb al-quẓāt* , ed. R. Guest (Leiden–London, 1912), p. 589.

3 al-Musabbiḥī, quoted by al-Maqrīzī, in *Khiṭaṭ*, vol. 1, p. 391, l. 1 ff.

4 al-Maqrīzī, *al-Khiṭaṭ*, vol. 2, p. 273, l. 27 ff.

5 Ibn Ḥajar al-ʿAsqalānī, *Rafʿ al-iṣr*, quoted in al-Kindī, *Kitāb al-wulāt*, p. 596, l. 19.

6 al-Maqrīzī, *Ittiʿāẓ*, vol. 1, p. 227; al-Kindī, *Kitāb al-wulāt*, p. 600; al-Qāḍī al-Nuʿmān's *Iqtiṣār* has been edited by M. Waḥīd Mīrzā (Damascus, 1957).

7 al-Maqrīzī, *al-Khiṭaṭ*, vol. 1, p. 391, l. 19 ff.

8 al-Maqrīzī, *al-Khiṭaṭ*, vol. 1, p. 425 ff.

9 Aḥmad b. ʿAlī al-Qalqashandī, *Ṣubḥ al-aʿshā*, (Cairo, 1331–38/1913–20), vol. 10, p. 37.

10 al-Maqrīzī, *Ittiʿāẓ*, vol. 2, p. 50, lines 9–15.

11 The printed text has: *wa-akhdh al-daʿwa ʿalāʾl-nās* ; perhaps it should be read: *wa-akhdh al-ʿahdʿalāʾl-nās* .

12 Quoted by al-Maqrīzī, *al-Khiṭaṭ*, vol. 1, p. 391 (= Ibn al-Ṭuwayr, *Nuzhat al-muqlatayn fi akhbār al-dawlatayn*, ed. A. Fuʾād Sayyid, Beirut, 1992, pp. 110–12).

13 Abuʾl-Qāsim Ismāʿīl al-Bustī, *Kashf asrār al-Bāṭiniyya*, Ms. Ambrosian Library, Milan, and H. Halm, *Kosmologie und Heilslehre der frühen Ismāʿīlīya* (Wiesbaden, 1978), pp. 129 ff. and 222–4.

14 See, for instance, Paul E. Walker, *Early Philosophical Shiism: The Ismaili Neoplatonism of Abū Yaʿqūb al-Sijistānī* (Cambridge, 1993), and his *Abū Yaʿqūb al-Sijistānī: Intellectual Missionary*, Ismaili Heritage Series, 1 (London, 1996).

15 Daniel De Smet, *La quiétude de l'intellect: Néoplatonisme et gnose ismaélienne dans l'oeuvre de Ḥamīd ad-Dīn al-Kirmānī* (Louvain, 1995).

Chapter 5

1 W. Ivanow, 'The Organization of the Fatimid Propaganda', *Journal of the Bombay Branch of the Royal Asiatic Society*, New Series, 15 (1939), p. 20.

2 al-Naysābūrī, *al-Risāla al-mūjaza*, facsimile edition, in Klemm, *Die Mission des fāṭimidischen Agenten*, p. 239.

Chapter 6

1 al-Maqrīzī, *al-Khiṭaṭ*, vol. 1, pp. 458 ff.
2 Ibid., vol. 1, p. 459.
3 Ibid.
4 al-Maqrīzī, *Ittiʿāẓ*, vol. 2, pp. 294 ff.
5 Ibid., vol. 2, p. 295.

Chapter 7

1 See al-Nuwayrī, *Nihāyat al-arab*, vol. 25, p. 205.
2 al-Maqrīzī, *al-Khiṭaṭ*, vol. 1, pp. 459 ff.
3 Ibid., vol. 1, p. 460.
4 Idrīs ʿImād al-Dīn,*ʿUyūn al-akhbār*, vol. 5, p. 105, also in Stern, *Studies in Early Ismāʿīlism*, p. 105.
5 al-Qāḍī al-Nuʿmān, *al-Majālis wa'l-musāyarāt*, pp. 131 ff.
6 al-Maqrīzī, *Ittiʿāẓ*, vol. 2, p. 100.
7 Ibn Taghrībirdī, *al-Nujūm al-zāhira fi mulūk Miṣr wa'l-Qāhira* (Cairo, 1348–1391/1929–72), vol. 4, p. 152.
8 al-Maqrīzī, *Ittiʿāẓ*, vol. 2, pp. 95, 117.
9 al-Maqrīzī, *al-Khiṭaṭ*, vol. 1, pp. 125–8.
10 al-Maqrīzī, *al-Khiṭaṭ*, vol. 1, p. 127.
11 al-Qāḍī al-Nuʿmān, *al-Majālis wa'l-musāyarāt*, p. 132.
12 Ibid., p. 533.
13 Quoted in al-Maqrīzī, *al-Khiṭaṭ*, vol. 1, p. 409.

Epilogue

1 ʿAṭā Malik Juwaynī, *The History of the World-Conqueror*, tr. John A. Boyle (Manchester, 1958), vol. 2, p. 719.

∞ Select Bibliography ∞

'Abd al-Jabbār b. Aḥmad al-Hamadhānī, al-Qāḍī. *Tathbīt dalā'il al-nubuwwa*, ed. 'A. 'Uthmān. Beirut, 1966.

al-'Awwā, 'Ādil, ed. *Muntakhabāt Ismā'īliyya.* Damascus, 1958.

Bianquis, Thierry. 'La prise du pouvoir par les Fatimides en Égypte (357–363/968–974)', *Annales Islamologiques*, 11 (1972), pp. 49–108.

_____ *Damas et la Syrie sous la domination Fatimide (359–468/969–1076).* Damascus, 1986–1989.

Canard, Marius. 'Fāṭimids', in *The Encyclopaedia of Islam*. New ed., Leiden–London, 1960 –, vol. 2, pp. 850–62.

_____ *Miscellanea Orientalia.* London, 1973.

Corbin, Henri. 'L'initiation ismaélienne ou l'ésotérisme et le Verbe', *Eranos Jahrbuch*, 39 (1970), pp. 41–142, reprinted in H. Corbin, *L'Homme et son ange.* Paris, 1983, pp. 81–205.

_____ 'Un roman initiatique ismaélien', *Cahiers de Civilisation Médiévale*, 15 (1972), pp. 1–25, 121–42.

Dachraoui, Farhat. *Le califat Fatimide au Maghreb (296–365 H./909–975 J.C.): Histoire politique et institutions.* Tunis, 1981.

Daftary, Farhad. *The Ismā'īlīs: Their History and Doctrines.* Cambridge, 1990.

_____ ed. *Mediaeval Isma'ili History and Thought.* Cambridge, 1996.

Ess, Josef van. *Chiliastische Erwartungen und die Versuchung der Göttlichkeit. Der Kalif al-Ḥākim (386–411 H.).* Heidelberg, 1977.

Fyzee, Asaf A. A. 'Qadi an-Nu'man: The Fatimid Jurist and Author', *Journal of the Royal Asiatic Society* (1934), pp. 1–32.

Ghālib, Muṣṭafā, ed. *Arba' kutub ḥaqqāniyya.* Beirut, 1987.

Halm, Heinz. *Kosmologie und Heilslehre der frühen Ismā'īlīya: Eine Studie zur islamischen Gnosis.* Wiesbaden, 1978.

_____ 'Les Fatimides à Salamya', *Revue des Études Islamiques*, 54 (1986), pp. 133–49.

_____ 'Der Treuhänder Gottes. Die Edikte des Kalifen al-Ḥākim', *Der Islam*, 63 (1986), pp. 11–72.

_____ 'Zwei fāṭimidische Quellen aus der Zeit des Kalifen al-Mahdī (909–34)', *Die Welt des Orients*, 19 (1988), pp. 102–17.

_____ 'Die Fatimiden', in U. Haarmann, ed., *Geschichte der arabischen Welt*. Munich, 1991, pp. 166–99, 605–6, 635–8.

_____ *Das Reich des Mahdi: Der Aufstieg der Fatimiden (875–973)*. Munich, 1991. English trans. *The Empire of the Mahdi: The Rise of the Fatimids*, tr. M. Bonner. Leiden, 1996.

_____ 'Al-Azhar, Dār al-'Ilm, al-Raṣad: Forschungs - und Lehranstalten der Fatimiden in Kairo', in U. Vermeulen and D. De Smet, eds, *Egypt and Syria in the Fatimid, Ayyubid and Mamluk Eras*. Louvain, 1995, pp. 99–109.

_____ 'The Isma'ili Oath of Allegiance (*'ahd*) and the Sessions of Wisdom (*majālis al-ḥikma*) in Fatimid Times', in F. Daftary, ed., *Mediaeval Isma'ili History and Thought*, pp. 91–115.

Ibn 'Idhārī, Abu'l-'Abbās Aḥmad. *al-Bayān al-mughrib*, ed. G. S. Colin and E. Lévi-Provençal. New ed., Leiden, 1948–1951.

Ibn Khallikān, Abu'l-'Abbās Aḥmad. *Wafayāt al-a'yān*, ed. I. 'Abbās. Beirut, 1968–1972.

Ibn Taghrībirdī, Abu'l-Maḥāsin Yūsuf. *al-Nujūm al-zāhira fī mulūk Miṣr wa'l-Qāhira*. Cairo, 1348–1391/1929–1972.

Ibn al-Ṭuwayr, Abū Muḥammad al-Murtaḍā. *Nuzhat al-muqlatayn fī akhbār al-dawlatayn*, ed. A. Fu'ād Sayyid. Beirut, 1992.

Idrīs 'Imād al-Dīn b. al-Hasan. *'Uyūn al-akhbār wa-funūn al-āthār*, vols 5 and 6, ed. M. Ghālib. Beirut, 1975–1984.

al-Imad, Leila S. *The Fatimid Vizierate, 969–1172*. Berlin, 1990.

Ivanow, Wladimir. 'The Organization of the Fatimid Propaganda', *Journal of the Bombay Branch of the Royal Asiatic Society*, New Series, 15 (1939), pp. 1–35.

_____ *Ismaili Tradition Concerning the Rise of the Fatimids*. London, etc., 1942.

_____ *The Alleged Founder of Ismailism*. Bombay, 1946.

_____ *Studies in Early Persian Ismailism*. 2nd ed., Bombay, 1955.

_____ *Ismaili Literature: A Bibliographical Survey*. Tehran, 1963.

Juwaynī, 'Aṭā Malik b. Muḥammad. *Ta'rīkh-i jahān-gushāy*, ed. M. Qazwīnī. Leiden–London, 1912–1937. English trans. John A. Boyle, *The History of the World-Conqueror*. Manchester, 1958.

al-Kindī, Abū 'Umar Muḥammad. *Kitāb al-wulāt wa-kitāb al-quḍāt*, ed. R. Guest. Leiden–London, 1912.

al-Kirmānī, Ḥamīd al-Dīn Aḥmad. *Kitāb al-riyāḍ*, ed. 'Ārif Tāmir. Beirut, 1960.

_____ *Rāḥat al-'aql*, ed. M. Kāmil Ḥusayn and M. Muṣṭafā Ḥilmī. Leiden-Cairo, 1953; ed. M. Ghālib. Beirut, 1967.

_____ *Majmūʿat rasāʾil*, ed. M. Ghālib. Beirut, 1983.

Kitāb al-ʿālim waʾl-ghulām, ed. M. Ghālib, in his *Arbaʿ kutub ḥaqqāniyya*, pp. 13–75. Abridged English trans. Ivanow, in his *Studies in Early Persian Ismailism*, pp. 61–86.

Klemm, Verena. *Die Mission des fāṭimidischen Agenten al-Muʾayyad fī d-dīn in Šīrāz*. Frankfurt, 1989.

Köhler, Bärbel. *Die Wissenschaft unter den ägyptischen Fatimiden*. Hildesheim, 1994.

Lev, Yaacov. 'The Fatimid Vizier Yaʿqūb ibn Killis and the Beginning of the Fatimid Administration in Egypt', *Der Islam*, 58 (1981), pp. 237–49.

_____ 'The Fāṭimid Princess Sitt al-Mulk', *Journal of Semitic Studies*, 32 (1987), pp. 319–28.

_____ 'The Fāṭimid Imposition of Ismāʿīlism on Egypt (358–386/969–996)', *Zeitschrift der Deutschen Morgenländischen Gesellschaft*, 138 (1988), pp. 313–25.

_____ *State and Society in Fatimid Egypt*. Leiden, 1991.

Lewis, Bernard. 'Ismāʿīlī Notes', *Bulletin of the School of Oriental and African Studies*, 12 (1947–1948), pp. 597–600.

Madelung, Wilferd. 'Ismāʿīliyya', in *The Encyclopaedia of Islam*. New ed., 1960 -, vol. 4, pp. 198–206.

al-Maqrīzī, Taqī al-Dīn Aḥmad. *Ittiʿāẓ al-ḥunafāʾ bi-akhbār al-aʾimma al-Fāṭimiyyīn al-khulafāʾ*, ed. J. al-Shayyāl and M. Ḥ. M. Aḥmad. Cairo, 1967–1973.

_____ *Kitāb al-mawāʿiẓ waʾl-iʿtibār bi-dhikr al-khiṭaṭ waʾl-āthār*. Būlāq, 1270/1853–1854.

_____ *Kitāb al-muqaffā al-kabīr*, ed. M. al-Yaʿlāwī. Beirut, 1991.

al-Muʾayyad fiʾl-Dīn al-Shīrāzī, Abū Naṣr Hibat Allāh. *al-Majālis al-Muʾayyadiyya*, vols 1 and 3, ed. M. Ghālib. Beirut, 1974–1984.

_____ *Sīra*, ed. M. Kāmil Ḥusayn. Cairo, 1949.

Nāṣir-i Khusraw. *Book of Travels (Safarnāma)*, tr. W. M. Thackston, Jr. Albany, N.Y., 1986.

al-Naysābūrī, Aḥmad b. Ibrāhīm. *Istitār al-imām*, ed. W. Ivanow, in *Bulletin of the Faculty of Arts, University of Egypt*, 4, part 2 (1936), pp. 93–107. English trans. W. Ivanow, in his *Ismaili Tradition Concerning the Rise of the Fatimids*, pp. 157–83.

al-Nuʿmān b. Muḥammad, al-Qāḍī Abū Ḥanīfa. *Daʿāʾim al-Islām*, ed. A. A. A. Fyzee. Cairo, 1951–1961. Partial English trans. Asaf A. A. Fyzee, *The Book of Faith*, Bombay, 1974.

_____ *Iftitāḥ al-daʿwa*, ed. W. al-Qāḍī. Beirut, 1970; ed. F. al-Dashrāwī. Tunis, 1975.

_____ *Kitāb al-himma fī ādāb atbāʿ al-aʾimma*, ed. M. Kāmil Ḥusayn. Cairo, n.d. [1948].

_____ *Kitāb al-iqtiṣār*, ed. M. Waḥīd Mīrzā. Damascus, 1957.

_____ *al-Majālis wa'l-musāyarāt*, ed. Ḥ. al-Faqī et al. Tunis, 1978.

_____ *Ta'wīl al-da'ā'im*, ed. M. Ḥ. al-A'ẓamī. Cairo, 1967–1972.

al-Nuwayrī, Shihāb al-Dīn Aḥmad. *Nihāyat al-arab fī funūn al-adab*, vol. 25, ed. M. J. 'A. al-Ḥīnī and 'A. al-Ahwānī. Cairo, 1984.

Poonawala, Ismail K. 'Al-Qāḍī al-Nu'mān's Works and the Sources', *Bulletin of the School of Oriental and African Studies*, 36 (1973), pp. 109–15.

_____ *Biobibliography of Ismā'īlī Literature*. Malibu, Calif., 1977.

_____ 'Al-Qāḍī al-Nu'mān and Isma'ili Jurisprudence', in F. Daftary, ed., *Mediaeval Isma'ili History and Thought*, pp. 117–43.

al-Qalqashandī, Shihāb al-Dīn Aḥmad. *Ṣubḥ al-a'shā*. Cairo, 1331–1338/1913–1920.

Raymond, André. *Le Caire*. Paris, 1993.

Sanders, Paula. *Ritual, Politics, and the City in Fatimid Cairo*. Albany, N.Y., 1994.

Sayyid, Ayman Fu'ād. *al-Dawla al-Fāṭimiyya fī Misr: Tafsīr jadīd*. Cairo, 1992.

Smet, Daniel De. *La quiétude de l'intellect: Néoplatonisme et gnose ismaélienne dans l'oeuvre de Ḥamīd ad-Dīn al-Kirmānī*. Louvain, 1995.

Stern, Samuel M. 'Cairo as the Centre of the Ismā'īlī Movement', in *Colloque international sur l'histoire du Caire*. Cairo, 1972, pp. 437–50.

_____ *Studies in Early Ismā'īlism*. Jerusalem-Leiden, 1983.

Walker, Paul E. *Early Philosophical Shiism: The Ismaili Neoplatonism of Abū Ya'qūb al-Sijistānī*. Cambridge, 1993.

_____ 'The Ismaili Da'wa in the Reign of the Fatimid Caliph al-Ḥākim', *Journal of the American Research Center in Egypt*, 30 (1993), pp. 161–82.

_____ *The Wellsprings of Wisdom: A Study of Abū Ya'qūb al-Sijistānī's Kitāb al-Yanābī'*. Salt Lake City, 1994.

_____ *Abū Ya'qūb al-Sijistānī: Intellectual Missionary*. Ismaili Heritage Series, 1. London, 1996.

al-Yamānī, Muḥammad b. Muḥammad. *Sīrat al-Ḥājib Ja'far b. 'Alī*, ed. W. Ivanow, in *Bulletin of the Faculty of Arts, University of Egypt*, 4, part 2 (1936), pp. 107–33. English trans. W. Ivanow, in his *Ismaili Tradition Concerning the Rise of the Fatimids*, pp. 184–223. French trans. M. Canard, 'L'autobiographie d'un chambellan du Mahdı 'Obeidallāh le Fāṭimide', *Hespéris*, 39 (1952), pp. 279–324, reprinted in his *Miscellanea Orientalia*, article V.

∞ Index ∞